CSWE EPAS 2008 Core Competencies

Professional Identity

2.1.1 Identify as a professional social worker and conduct oneself accordingly.

Necessary Knowledge, Values, Skills

- Social workers serve as representatives of the profession, its mission, and its core values.
- Social workers know the profession's history.
- Social workers commit themselves to the profession's enhancement and to their own professional conduct and growth.

Operational Practice Behaviors

- Social workers advocate for client access to the services of social work;
- Social workers practice personal reflection and self-correction to assure continual professional development;
- Social workers attend to professional roles and boundaries;
- Social workers demonstrate professional demeanor in behavior, appearance, and communication;
- Social workers engage in career-long learning; and
- Social workers use supervision and consultation.

Ethical Practice

2.1.2 Apply social work ethical principles to guide professional practice.

Necessary Knowledge, Values, Skills

- Social workers have an obligation to conduct themselves ethically and engage in ethical decision-making.
- Social workers are knowledgeable about the value base of the profession, its ethical standards, and relevant law.

Operational Practice Behaviors

- Social workers recognize and manage personal values in a way that allows professional values to guide practice;
- Social workers make ethical decisions by applying standards of the National Association of Social Workers Code of Ethics and, as applicable, of the International Federation of Social Workers/International Association of Schools of Social Work Ethics in Social Work, Statement of Principles;
- Social workers tolerate ambiguity in resolving ethical conflicts; and
- Social workers apply strategies of ethical reasoning to arrive at principled decisions.

Critical Thinking

2.1.3 Apply critical thinking to inform and communicate professional judgments.

Necessary Knowledge, Values, Skills

- Social workers are knowledgeable about the principles of logic, scientific inquiry, and reasoned discernment.
- They use critical thinking augmented by creativity and curiosity.
- Critical thinking also requires the synthesis and communication of relevant information.

Operational Practice Behaviors

- Social workers distinguish, appraise, and integrate multiple sources of knowledge, including research-based knowledge, and practice wisdom;
- Social workers analyze models of assessment, prevention, intervention, and evaluation; and
- Social workers demonstrate effective oral and written communication in working with individuals, families, groups, organizations, communities, and colleagues.

Adapted with the permission of Council on Social Work Education

Diversity in Practice
2.1.4 Engage diversity and difference in practice.

Necessary Knowledge, Values, Skills

- Social workers understand how diversity characterizes and shapes the human experience and is critical to the formation of identity.
- The dimensions of diversity are understood as the intersectionality of multiple factors including age, class, color, culture, disability, ethnicity, gender, gender identity and expression, immigration status, political ideology, race, religion, sex, and sexual orientation.
- Social workers appreciate that, as a consequence of difference, a person's life experiences may include oppression, poverty, marginalization, and alienation as well as privilege, power, and acclaim.

Operational Practice Behaviors

- Social workers recognize the extent to which a culture's structures and values may oppress, marginalize, alienate, or create or enhance privilege and power;
- Social workers gain sufficient self-awareness to eliminate the influence of personal biases and values in working with diverse groups;
- Social workers recognize and communicate their understanding of the importance of difference in shaping life experiences; and
- Social workers view themselves as learners and engage those with whom they work as informants.

Human Rights & Justice
2.1.5 Advance human rights and social and economic justice.

Necessary Knowledge, Values, Skills

- Each person, regardless of position in society, has basic human rights, such as freedom, safety, privacy, an adequate standard of living, health care, and education.
- Social workers recognize the global interconnections of oppression and are knowledgeable about theories of justice and strategies to promote human and civil rights.
- Social work incorporates social justice practices in organizations, institutions, and society to ensure that these basic human rights are distributed equitably and without prejudice.

Operational Practice Behaviors

- Social workers understand the forms and mechanisms of oppression and discrimination;
- Social workers advocate for human rights and social and economic justice; and
- Social workers engage in practices that advance social and economic justice.

Research Based Practice
2.1.6 Engage in research-informed practice and practice-informed research.

Necessary Knowledge, Values, Skills

- Social workers use practice experience to inform research, employ evidence-based interventions, evaluate their own practice, and use research findings to improve practice, policy, and social service delivery.
- Social workers comprehend quantitative and qualitative research and understand scientific and ethical approaches to building knowledge.

Operational Practice Behaviors

- Social workers use practice experience to inform scientific inquiry; and
- Social workers use research evidence to inform practice.

Human Behavior
2.1.7 Apply knowledge of human behavior and the social environment.

Necessary Knowledge, Values, Skills

- Social workers are knowledgeable about human behavior across the life course; the range of social systems in which people live; and the ways social systems promote or deter people in maintaining or achieving health and well-being.
- Social workers apply theories and knowledge from the liberal arts to understand biological, social, cultural, psychological, and spiritual development.

Operational Practice Behaviors

- Social workers utilize conceptual frameworks to guide the processes of assessment, intervention, and evaluation; and
- Social workers critique and apply knowledge to understand person and environment.

Policy Practice   2.1.8 Engage in policy practice to advance social and economic well-being and to deliver effective social work services.

Necessary Knowledge, Values, Skills

- Social work practitioners understand that policy affects service delivery and they actively engage in policy practice.
- Social workers know the history and current structures of social policies and services; the role of policy in service delivery; and the role of practice in policy development.

Operational Practice Behaviors

- Social workers analyze, formulate, and advocate for policies that advance social well-being; and
- Social workers collaborate with colleagues and clients for effective policy action.

Practice Contexts

2.1.9 Respond to contexts that shape practice.

Necessary Knowledge, Values, Skills

- Social workers are informed, resourceful, and proactive in responding to evolving organizational, community, and societal contexts at all levels of practice.
- Social workers recognize that the context of practice is dynamic, and use knowledge and skill to respond proactively.

Operational Practice Behaviors

- Social workers continuously discover, appraise, and attend to changing locales, populations, scientific and technological developments, and emerging societal trends to provide relevant services; and
- Social workers provide leadership in promoting sustainable changes in service delivery and practice to improve the quality of social services.

Engage, Assess, Intervene, Evaluate   2.1.10 Engage, assess, intervene, and evaluate with individuals, families, groups, organizations, and communities.

Necessary Knowledge, Values, Skills

- Professional practice involves the dynamic and interactive processes of engagement, assessment, intervention, and evaluation at multiple levels.
- Social workers have the knowledge and skills to practice with individuals, families, groups, organizations, and communities.
- Practice knowledge includes
  - identifying, analyzing, and implementing evidence-based interventions designed to achieve client goals;
  - using research and technological advances;
  - evaluating program outcomes and practice effectiveness;
  - developing, analyzing, advocating, and providing leadership for policies and services; and
  - promoting social and economic justice.

Operational Practice Behaviors

(a) Engagement

- Social workers substantively and affectively prepare for action with individuals, families, groups, organizations, and communities;
- Social workers use empathy and other interpersonal skills; and
- Social workers develop a mutually agreed-on focus of work and desired outcomes.

(b) Assessment

- Social workers collect, organize, and interpret client data;
- Social workers assess client strengths and limitations;
- Social workers develop mutually agreed-on intervention goals and objectives; and
- Social workers select appropriate intervention strategies.

(c) Intervention

- Social workers initiate actions to achieve organizational goals;
- Social workers implement prevention interventions that enhance client capacities;
- Social workers help clients resolve problems;
- Social workers negotiate, mediate, and advocate for clients; and
- Social workers facilitate transitions and endings.

(d) Evaluation

- Social workers critically analyze, monitor, and evaluate interventions.

Connecting Core Competencies

A Workbook for Social Work Students

Quienton Nichols
Kennesaw State University

Allyn & Bacon
Boston   Columbus   Indianapolis   New York   San Francisco   Upper Saddle River
Amsterdam   Cape Town   Dubai   London   Madrid   Milan   Munich   Paris   Montreal   Toronto
Delhi   Mexico City   São Paulo   Sydney   Hong Kong   Seoul   Singapore   Taipei   Tokyo

Editorial Director: Craig Campanella
Editor in Chief: Dickson Musslewhite
Executive Editor: Ashley Dodge
Editorial Product Manager: Carly Czech
Director of Marketing: Brandy Dawson
Executive Marketing Manager: Jeanette Koskinas
Senior Marketing Manager: Wendy Albert
Marketing Assistant: Shauna Fishweicher
Lead Media Project Manager: Thomas Scalzo
Managing Editor: Maureen Richardson

Senior Project Manager/Liaison: Harriet Tellem
Senior Operations Specialist: Sherry Lewis
Text Design: PreMediaGlobal
Art Director, Cover: Jayne Conte
Cover Designer: Bruce Kenselaar
Full-Service Project Management: Marie Desrosiers/PreMediaGlobal
Composition: PreMediaGlobal
Printer/Binder: Bind-Rite Graphics
Cover Printer: Lehigh-Phoenix Color

Credits and acknowledgments borrowed from other sources and reproduced, with permission, in this textbook appear on appropriate page within text (or on page 153).

Library of Congress Cataloging-in-Publication Data

Nichols, Quienton.
　Connecting core competencies : a work book for social work students / Quienton Nichols.
　　p. cm.
　Includes bibliographical references.
　ISBN 978-0-205-01246-6
1. Social service.　2. Social work education.　3. Evidence-based social work.　4. Core competencies.
5. Professional ethics.　I. Title.
　HV40.N53 2012
　361.3—dc22

2010042368

10 9 8 7 6 5 4 3 2 1

Allyn & Bacon
is an imprint of

PEARSON

www.pearsonhighered.com

Student Edition:
ISBN-10: 0-205-01246-9
ISBN-13: 978-0-205-01246-6

à la Carte Edition:
ISBN-10: 0-205-01369-4
ISBN-13: 978-0-205-01369-2

CONTENTS

INTRODUCTION

The Council on Social Work Education (CSWE) is a nonprofit national association representing more than 3,000 individual members, as well as graduate and undergraduate programs of professional social work education. Founded in 1952, this partnership of educational and professional institutions, social welfare agencies, and private citizens is recognized by the Council for Higher Education Accreditation as the sole accrediting agency for social work education in the United States. Social work schools and departments focus on the CSWE Educational Policy and Accreditation Standards (EPAS) to guide their accreditation process. The current standards, approved in June 2008, focus on the mastery of ten core competencies and 40 practice behaviors. These ten core competencies provide specific knowledge, values, skills, and resulting practice behaviors that guide the curriculum and assessment methods of all social work programs (CSWE, 2010).

This workbook will focus on the foundation curriculum using the 2008 Educational Policy and Accreditation Standards (EPAS). The first-year foundation focuses on generalist practices that will prepare you to analyze problems holistically and design, as well as plan, interventions aimed at multiple levels of systems that respond to client problems. The first-year foundation further prepares students for practice behaviors for the advanced second-year concentration or specialization. The 2008 EPAS defines ten competencies, EP 2.1.1–EP 2.1.10(d), and moves social work to a competency-based outcomes approach to social work education that ensures that students graduate with the knowledge, values, and skills that define what social workers must be able to apply in practice as professionals.

HOW TO USE THIS WORKBOOK

This workbook is intended to build upon your prior knowledge gained from previous social work courses as well as to present an overview of generalist practice and principles related to the core competencies. It also provides a detailed understanding and explanation of each EPAS standard and is followed by questions that are divided into categories: (1) Understanding of Knowledge and (2) Mastery and Assessment of Knowledge of Skills. The questions that represent understanding of knowledge are multiple-choice questions and require you to select the *best* answer from among the possible choices. The questions that represent mastery and assessment of knowledge of skills are multiple-choice, essay, and case vignettes and require the application of your learning of each EPAS standard. All question types will be found throughout the workbook.

CHAPTER STRUCTURE

Although the chapters are numbered, this does not suggest that you move through the workbook sequentially. The workbook is written so that you can move back and forth between sections and focus on a particular core competency as appropriate. You may even wish to revisit certain core competencies as needed. Chapters are arranged by the Educational Policy numbers, beginning with 2.1.1 Professional Identity and ending with 2.1.10(a)–(d): Engage, Assess, Intervene, Evaluate.

Each numbered EPAS will be defined under the Detailed Understanding and Explanation, so as to help you develop a clear understanding of each core competency. The concepts and definitions presented should serve as a review of key ideas that will stimulate critical thinking and raise other important social work questions.

1

PROFESSIONAL IDENTITY

DETAILED UNDERSTANDING AND EXPLANATION (DUE)

Your social work education will teach you to understand the profession's history, mission, values, and ethics and will serve as a foundation in the development of your professional identity. Social work has a rich history. Though it may appear that its past does not relate to today's society given the technological advances and global world in which we live, it is important to note that historical events have shaped our current thinking, policy development, practice methods, and evaluation procedures. To understand social work today, you must understand its history. Many forces and persons have shaped current social work practices. Many of the early social workers were highly regarded and recognized and their contributions helped to shape the "professional identity" of social work.

Your professional social work education will prepare you with the knowledge, skills, and values you will use to function effectively as a beginning social worker. For the first year of the MSW program, which is referred to as the foundation year, you will be prepared to do generalist practice. A few MSW programs are designed to prepare students for generalist practice during year one and advanced generalist practice for year two. However, most MSW programs prepare students for generalist practice during the first year and various specializations and concentrations (e.g., mental health, children and families, substance abuse, aging, and child welfare) during the second year. The first year will provide you with an integrated and multilevel approach which will prepare you to meet the needs of clients based on three major principles: (1) the person in the context of the environment, (2) the multilevel assessment process, and (3) social justice.

Your coursework will allow you to understand the client within the context of his or her social and physical environments, and based on the person-in-environment linkage, you will learn how to change systems and modify clients' interactions with the environment. Your first-year foundation courses will allow you to implement multilevel assessments and interventions in which you will learn to work with individuals, families, groups, organizations, neighborhoods, and communities that are richly diverse. You will connect clients to a wide range of resources that can provide them with needed goods and services while utilizing various social work roles. As social work students, you have responsibilities to work for social justice and the application of research to your practice. As you work with diverse clients, you will strive towards improving the quality of their lives by promoting policies and legislation that support social justice.

As a beginning social work student, you will learn the multiplicity of your identity and the diversity of your roles and responsibilities, particularly in your first year of field internship. These various identities include, but are not limited to: counselor/enabler, advocate, broker, case manager, educator, facilitator, organizer, mediator, negotiator, initiator, coordinator, researcher, and public speaker. These professional roles and identities shape and guide the actions that you, as social work interns, utilize in the field under the guidance of a supervisor. This section will discuss the different identities and/or roles of a professional social worker and speak to the practice behaviors associated with each role.

In the role of **counselor/enabler**, you will gain an understanding of how to empower clients and help them understand as well as cope with an array of thoughts and an assortment of feelings that they may be experiencing. You will learn to identify client strengths and to help them use these strengths to properly manage their problems. This, in turn, will improve clients' social functioning by: (1) helping to reduce or modify behaviors, (2) changing behavioral patterns in relationships, (3) assisting in learning how to deal with forces in their social and physical environments that require change, and (4) assisting in learning how to engage differentially with these environments.

In the role of **advocate**, you will assist clients in fighting for their rights as well as the rights of others to obtain needed resources. You will learn to advocate for your clients by talking and/or consulting with other social workers and professionals such as doctors, judges, teachers, housing personnel, and medical staff on behalf of your clients. When you speak with a landlord on behalf of a client and arrange for that landlord to allow your client to pay his or her rent two weeks later than required, you have successfully advocated on that client's behalf. Advocacy can also be employed in support of large groups of people or for political purposes. When you write letters to state and national congressmen in support of bills and policies that will enhance the lives of all people, including the clients you serve, you are demonstrating advocacy efforts. Additionally, when you meet with legislators to discuss legislation in support of client needs (need for recreational facilities to be open during summers, more stringent laws against men who use teenage females as prostitutes, and the need for more homeless shelters), you are developing advocacy skills.

The role of **broker** is very similar to the role of advocate with the exception that it requires less assertive and aggressive action. The role of broker involves referring an individual client or family to other supportive resources and, when appropriate, following up to ensure that the client receives them. For example, a mother with several children in middle school may not be knowledgeable about various services that are available to her children such as the Big Brother program, YWCA, mentoring programs offered at the local school or at various colleges and universities, and services offered by agencies for middle school children. Your knowledge of such services might include understanding eligibility requirements, and whether the services are free or have a fee or if services are means-tested and/or possibly based on a sliding scale. In the role of broker, your knowledge of services will be important and will empower you to serve clients in this role.

The **case manager** role involves planning, locating, and securing services for clients who are not able to do so due to a physical or mental impairment, mental illness, age, etc. You can locate these services for clients so they can benefit from them. By and large, the case manager role entails some counseling in that it involves engaging clients in discussing issues impacting them and possible services that are available to them. The case manager role may be brief or long-term depending on the client's needs, and could involve referral, follow-up, and monitoring of such services. As a case manager you may also have to ensure that clients receive quality care.

Your role as an **educator** is as the word implies—to teach clients about services and resources that are available and how to use and access them. In addition, your role as educator can teach parents effective parenting skills, educate couples about better communication skills, and train families on how to identify dysfunctional patterns that may exist within the family system. As an educator, you will be able to assist clients in employing methods on how to change dysfunctional patterns in the interest of becoming healthier, happier people. The educator role may also serve to assist teachers in better understanding children's behaviors and ways they can help children within the context of the classroom.

The **facilitator** role is often used when one is working with groups. In this role you will be able to establish groups for specific purposes, engage group members, and make interventions that support group members individually and collectively. As a group facilitator, you will be able to lead various groups to include a therapy group, an educational group, a self-help group, or a group focused on clients who have or are experiencing similar problems, such as children whose parents are divorced or children who have experienced the loss of a parent.

The social worker as **organizer** will bring together members of other agencies to discuss issues that impact clients from various agencies. For example, if a bus service that serves clients from several agencies is discontinued, a social worker from one agency may bring social workers from other agencies together to discuss the issue of transportation and help find a short-term solution while working toward a more long-term resolution. The short-term solution may be to help organize a "car pool" to get clients to and from work. Bringing together members of the community (board of transportation members, politicians, agency representatives, churches, and other community representatives) will lead to a more long-term solution to the transportation needs of the community residents. The organizer role can be used to bring about policy changes within an agency or at the local, state, or national levels.

Your roles as a mediator, negotiator, initiator, and/or coordinator are important for you as a first-year student to understand. The role of **mediator** will allow you to intervene in disputes between parties so that they can find compromises, reconcile differences, or reach agreements—this role is often a part of the counseling role—while the role of **negotiator** is to bring together persons who are in conflict so that a bargain or compromise can be agreed upon and implemented. Your role as **initiator** will entail calling attention to a problem that was not seen initially and helping the client address the particular problem or concern. As **coordinator**, you will bring together different agencies, units, or members of a family in an effort to work on shared goals.

You, as a first-year social work student, must also understand your role as a **researcher**. You must be able to select interventions such that you can monitor the progress of your clients and evaluate their effectiveness. You will also learn to conduct research in the classroom and in your work with clients. This evidence-based process will ensure that you are accountable to your clients and the larger public. Being a researcher will also entail your being able to critique literature on particular clinical topics so that your practice will be current and "cutting edge."

You will also assume the role of **public speaker**, where you will be asked to talk with groups of people about different issues such as the misuse of technology by children and adolescents, bullying, date violence, teen pregnancy, and neighborhood gangs, as well as being asked to address parent groups, police officers, and agency staff. Various organizations, community groups, and schools recognize the important areas of expertise you are knowledgeable about, and will want to have you share your knowledge on a number of topics.

You are encouraged to join professional organizations, such as NASW and Clinical Social Work Societies, as student members so that you are able to learn more about the profession. You are also encouraged to attend the Council on Social Work Education Annual Program Meetings (APM), where you will meet social work educators, many of whom have written the books from which you are learning and are experts in the field. Attendance at these meetings will further expose you to the social work profession. This will help to enhance and strengthen your professional identity. The academic experiences, field internships, and attendance at professional meetings and conferences will allow you to fully immerse yourself in the process of developing your identity as a professional social worker.

The social work roles described above will help you begin to assume your professional identity as a social worker. As well, you will also learn during your first year what it means to be a social worker by observing your professors and agency supervisors, who serve as social work role models. For those of you who have prior social work experiences, your professional identity will already have begun to take shape. Those without experience will start to assume a beginning professional identity. However, each of you will begin the process of strengthening your identity as you learn within the classroom the history, mission, goals, ethics, and values of the profession and how to apply this knowledge in your field internship. These roles, learned in the first year, will be expanded upon during your second year of advanced specialization.

Generalist social work practices will allow you to work at three levels of intervention: (1) micro level, (2) mezzo level, and (3) macro level. Micro-level interventions will assist you in your work with individuals, families, and small groups. Mezzo-level interventions will allow you to create teams with organizations and the network of helping professional agencies. Macro-level interventions will allow you to intervene at the community, institutional, and societal levels.

UNDERSTANDING OF KNOWLEDGE

Please choose the *best* answer from among the possible choices.

1. The ability to empower the client and help him or her understand and manage an array of thoughts and feelings describes which social work role?

    a. Broker
    b. Educator
    c. Counselor/enabler
    d. Organizer

2. When a social worker assists clients in fighting for their rights as well as the rights of others to obtain needed resources, this role is known as:

    a. Educator
    b. Advocate
    c. Mediator
    d. Researcher

3. When a social worker brings together members of other agencies to discuss an issue that impacts clients in an effort to bring about policy changes within an agency or at a local or national level, he or she is acting as:

    a. Facilitator
    b. Organizer
    c. Mediator
    d. Negotiator

4. When a social worker teaches clients about available services and resources and how to use and access these services, he or she is acting in the role of:

   a. Educator
   b. Researcher
   c. Facilitator
   d. Case manager

5. When a social worker meets with legislators to discuss legislation in support of client needs, he or she is acting in the role of:

   a. Initiator
   b. Coordinator
   c. Researcher
   d. Advocate

6. When a social worker refers an individual client to other helpful resources and follows up to ensure that the needed resources are obtained, she or he is assuming the role of:

   a. Researcher
   b. Facilitator
   c. Broker
   d. Organizer

7. When a social worker writes letters or sends e-mails to state and national congressmen in support of bills and policies that will enhance the lives of all people, including the clients, he or she is:

   a. Demonstrating his or her brokerage skills
   b. Demonstrating advocacy efforts
   c. Revealing his or her ability to communicate in written form
   d. Indicating his or her ability to mediate for clients

8. In planning, locating, and securing services for clients who are not able to do so themselves due to a physical or mental impairment, mental illness, or age, the social worker is serving in the role of:

   a. Case manager
   b. Facilitator
   c. Organizer
   d. Educator

9. A social worker who teaches parents effective parenting skills, trains couples on better communication skills, and helps to change family dysfunctional patterns is serving in the role of:

   a. Mediator
   b. Educator
   c. Negotiator
   d. Initiator

10. The social worker who works with groups for specific purposes, to include interventions that support group members individually and collectively, is serving in the role of:

    a. Facilitator
    b. Negotiator
    c. Initiator
    d. Researcher

11. A social worker who intervenes in disputes between parties to bring about concessions, reconcile differences, and/or reach agreements is serving as:

    a. Negotiator
    b. Mediator
    c. Compromiser
    d. Public speaker

12. A social worker who brings together individuals who are in conflict so that a bargain or compromise can be agreed upon and implemented is serving as:

    a. Negotiator
    b. Educator
    c. Compromiser
    d. Public speaker

13. A social worker who brings together different agencies, units, and/or members of a family in an effort to work on shared goals is serving in the role of:

    a. Negotiator
    b. Mediator
    c. Coordinator
    d. Public speaker

14. A social worker who leads various group experiences to include a therapy group, an educational group, a self-help group, or a group focused on clients who have or are experiencing similar problems is serving in the role of:

    a. Negotiator
    b. Facilitator
    c. Compromiser
    d. Public speaker

15. When a social worker links the community with the agency, he or she is serving in the role of:

    a. Advocate
    b. Broker
    c. Counselor
    d. Researcher

16. Mothers from a housing project want to work, but have no childcare. A social worker from the family agency has been assigned to work with the mothers. The mothers are aware that a child-care center in another town is interested in opening a child-care center in a different area. The social worker has invited the director of the child-care center to meet with her and several of the mothers. The social worker's role is that of:

    a. Educator
    b. Advocate
    c. Broker
    d. Enabler

17. If a social work student is serving as an intern, she should:

    a. Say she is a social worker.
    b. Identify herself as a student social worker doing an internship.
    c. Say she is a counselor.
    d. Say she is a psychologist.

18. The three levels of intervention used by generalist social workers are:

    a. Milieu, macro, and mezzo
    b. Macro, messo, and mecca
    c. Mesa, mezzo, and macro
    d. Micro, mezzo, and macro

19. A generalist social worker whose interventions focus on working with individuals, families, and small groups to foster change is working at which level?

    a. Mezzo
    b. Macro
    c. Micro
    d. Mecca

MASTERY AND ASSESSMENT OF
KNOWLEDGE OF SKILLS

Please choose the *best* answer from among the possible choices.

1. A social worker organizes a group of families who are indignant because persons who live outside the community are using a nearby vacant lot to dump garbage. The most effective strategy the social worker can employ is to:

   a. Send a list of demands to the city council.
   b. Select representatives to speak with the city council regarding removal of the garbage.
   c. Do nothing but continue to complain.
   d. Arrange a "sit-in" at the community center.

2. Several students at Crawford Middle School have experienced the death of a parent. Teachers are concerned that the students are demonstrating behaviors in response to the loss. The school social worker should:

   a. Meet with individual students who experienced the death.
   b. Consult with teachers and instruct them to speak with the students during class about their concerns.
   c. Contact a consultant to conduct a minimum of two sessions with all middle school students to discuss their feelings and make referrals of individual students as appropriate.
   d. Call a meeting with parents to discuss the deaths.

3. Jay is a social worker who is identifying as a mediator for LL Counseling. His most important role is to:

   a. Call attention to a problem that was not seen initially.
   b. Intervene in disputes between parties in an effort to reconcile differences and find compromises.
   c. Bring together members of agencies to discuss issues that impact clients.
   d. Establish groups for specific purposes.

4. The state legislature is considering the development of a walk and bike path that will be convenient for several neighborhoods and will serve all age groups. Several agencies are located in the different communities. A social worker at the family service agency agrees to coordinate a write-in campaign involving the surrounding communities in support of the "walk and bike path." The social worker's role is that of:

   a. Educator
   b. Advocate
   c. Mediator
   d. Organizer

5. The initiator's most important role is to:

a. Bring together members of agencies to discuss issues that impact clients.
b. Establish groups for specific purposes.
c. Call attention to a problem that was not seen initially and help the client address the particular problem or concern.
d. Intervene in disputes between parties in an effort to reconcile differences and find compromises.

6. You are identifying as a coordinator at QQ's Counseling Center. Your role is to:

a. Bring together members of agencies, units, or members of a family in an effort to work out shared goals that can be achieved by these units working together.
b. Establish groups for specific purposes.
c. Call attention to a problem that was not seen initially and help the client address the particular problem or concern.
d. Intervene in disputes between parties in an effort to reconcile differences and find compromises.

7. John Doe is a social worker for Helping Hands Transportation. He learns that the bus service that serves clients from several agencies is discontinued. He decides that it would be beneficial to bring together social workers from other agencies to discuss the issue in an effort to help find a short-term solution. John is most likely functioning in the role of:

a. Mediator
b. Initiator
c. Organizer
d. Case manager

8. An eight-year-old African American child is placed in a foster home with two other children, ages eleven and six. The child continuously fights the other children, and takes their toys and refuses to give them back. The eight-year-old child's social worker is contacted. Her first step should be to:

a. Evaluate the other children in the home for potential risk.
b. Have the foster mother attend a parenting class.
c. Remove the child from the home.
d. Place the child in a group home.

9. A child whose parents have recently separated is showing a great deal of anxiety and is "acting out" at school. The child lives with his mother. The social worker should:

a. Contact the mother and make a referral for mother and child.
b. Suspend the child for a few days and have the mother spend time with him.

    c. Contact the father.

    d. Begin counseling sessions with the child at school.

10. A social work student likes it that her teacher actively listens, engages the students, and treats them with respect. The social work student demonstrates this behavior at her agency internship with her clients when she:

    a. Shows anger at the client when she is late for an appointment

    b. Is culturally responsive, is accepting of the clients concerns, and responds sensitively

    c. Is constantly late for client appointments

    d. Shares information about the client with her friends

11. A social worker arranges with the public library a time for the elementary students to attend a special reading group on Saturday. The Smith family has a son, Joshua, whose many problems interfere with his ability to participate in the program. Joshua has a history of beating his classmates and using foul language. The social worker should:

    a. Meet with Ms. Smith to discuss Joshua's behavior and refer the family to an agency for counseling.

    b. Immediately provide counseling for Joshua.

    c. Advise the mother that Joshua should not attend the reading sessions.

    d. Discuss Joshua's behavior with the teachers.

12. Ms. Anderson is being seen by a family service agency for depression that is, in part, related to her husband's alcoholism. She is concerned that her husband's behavior, especially while drinking, is negatively impacting all family members. The social worker should:

    a. Contact AA and make appropriate referrals for all family members based on the discussion with the AA representative.

    b. Suggest that the husband join the wife in couples counseling.

    c. Suggest family therapy for the entire family.

    d. Continue to see the wife and allow her to talk through her concerns.

13. Ms. Jones is an African American single mother of four children: twin sons, age 14; a son, age 11; and a daughter, age 8. She is a good mother who works hard to ensure that her children attend and do well in school and participate in various community activities. Her community center offers a three-month jazz music program that provides instruments; however, each child is required to pay a monthly fee of $20. Her sons want to participate, but the fee is a challenge and she can only afford $25 per month for all of her children. The social worker gets the community agency to accept the $25 fee. In this role, the social worker serves as:

a. Educator
b. Advocate
c. Mediator
d. Researcher

14. You are an intern at ABC Family Counseling Center, where you are co-leading a group session led by your supervisor and two other interns from other universities. During the session, one of the interns provides useful suggestions to the group but does so with an agitated and angry tone of voice. The members become extremely displeased with the intern. The group leader should:

a. Ask each member of the group to point out what the intern did right and wrong.
b. Encourage the group to move on and then schedule a separate session with the intern.
c. Respond actively by identifying what the intern did well and then offer constructive feedback.
d. Do nothing and allow the group to "heal" on its own.

Reflective Essay Questions

1. What is the role of the Council on Social Work Education (CSWE)?

2. Discuss one example of how you have been able to advocate for a client.

3. Identify two persons (i.e., social workers, social work educators, former supervisors, or social work administrators) you know or have worked with who have served as social work role models for you. Give reasons why each person has served as your role model.

4. Explain the qualities demonstrated by persons you admire that you hope to make a part of your social work identity.

5. Identify the social work organization(s) in which you are currently a student member or hope to have student membership. Why is membership in this organization important?

2

ETHICAL PRACTICE

DETAILED UNDERSTANDING AND EXPLANATION (DUE)

Social work practice is guided by knowledge, skills, ethics, and values. The social work code of ethics is defined by the National Association of Social Workers. The NASW Code of Ethics forms the foundation of the profession's values in that it defines the principles and standards for everyday behaviors for all social workers. The Code of Ethics defines the ethical responsibilities social workers have to: (1) clients, (2) colleagues, (3) practice settings, (4) themselves as professionals, (5) the profession, and (6) the broader society (NASW Code of Ethics, revised by the 2008 NASW Delegate Assembly).

Occasionally, social workers are unable to distinguish between the terms values and ethics. In fact, sometimes the terms are used interchangeably; but they are not identical because they have different meanings. Social worker values are often taken from values held by the larger society. Values are concerned with "what is good and desirable, while ethics deal what is right and correct" (Dolgoff, Loewenberg, & Harrington, 2009). Values reflect very strong beliefs about how the world should be and how people should behave. Sometimes people interpret values in different ways that may be controversial. For example, people in the United States have different values about some issues which create large societal debates as seen in responses to abortion, gay and lesbian rights, gun control, affirmative action, minimum wage, and immigration, among others.

The NASW Code of Ethics provides broad ethical principles that are based on social work's core values: service and the importance of human relationships, social justice, dignity and worth of the person, integrity, and competence (NASW, 2010).

The service value for social workers means that service to others takes precedence above self-interest. Hence, social workers use their knowledge, skills, and values to help people who have varying needs. Within this value, social workers respect the human dignity of each individual and believe that each person is unique and has inherent worth. The service value espoused by social workers also recognizes the vital importance of human relationships. The relationship between social worker and client is essential to the social worker's ability to make interventions that support healthy functioning.

The value of social justice means that social workers will pursue and promote fair and equitable treatment for all persons including people of color and other vulnerable populations (e.g., elderly, gays and lesbians, women, homeless, etc). In this regard, you, as students, will promote social change that will result in enhanced economic, political, and societal advancement. Social justice also requires that you are culturally competent and sensitive to diversity and will promote the elimination of poverty and discrimination.

Social workers believe in the inherent dignity and worth of every individual and demonstrate this value through our relationships with others. We value diversity and work to ensure that all people are able to maximize their potential through the availability and accessibility of opportunities. In recognizing each person's dignity and worth, social workers support self-determination and the right of each individual to make his or her decisions.

Social workers value integrity and competence. Integrity supports basic honesty, truthfulness, and honor. In this regard, social workers should engage in ethical practice that reflects their responsibility to clients, colleagues, agencies, communities, and society. The NASW Code of Ethic states: "social workers practice within their areas of competence and develop and enhance their professional expertise" (NASW Code of Ethics, approved by the 1996 NASW Delegate Assembly and revised by the 2008 NASW Delegate Assembly). Under this ethical principle, social workers have the responsibility to value current knowledge and to see learning as a lifelong process. Competence as a value means that social workers will continue to refine their knowledge base to ensure that they are utilizing "cutting-edge" theories to support their assessments, interventions, diversity, and social justice.

Moving from values to action in one's behavior can be difficult. Dolgoff, Loewenberg, & Harrington (2009) define ethics as "that branch of philosophy that concerns itself with human conduct and moral decision making." Ethics serve to guide people in deciding what is right or wrong. The NASW Code of Ethics provides rules of conduct to which social workers must adhere if they are to remain in good standing within the profession. The Code provides responsibilities and behaviors that social workers must follow. As a student you must become familiar with the NASW Code of Ethics and should address any concerns regarding potential ethical violations with your supervisor. Even when you are in doubt with regard to a potential ethical violation, it is important that you share your concerns with your immediate supervisor to ensure that you are ethically responsible.

The social worker's key ethical responsibilities to clients as defined by the Code of Ethics (approved by the 1996 NASW Delegate Assembly and revised by the 2008 NASW Delegate Assembly) are as follows: commitment to clients, self-determination, informed consent, competence, cultural competence and social diversity, conflicts of interest, privacy and confidentiality, access to records, sexual relationships, physical contact, sexual harassment, derogatory language, payment for services, clients who lack decision-making capacity, and termination of services (NASW, 2008).

While all of the ethical responsibilities to clients are important and should be discussed by social work professors with students in their first year of foundation, this chapter will focus on four key ethical principles: (1) self-determination, (2) informed consent, (3) professional boundaries, and (4) confidentiality.

Self-Determination

Self-determination as defined by Suppes & Wells (2009) is "an ethical principle of the social work profession which recognizes the right and need of clients to make their own choices and decisions." The NASW Code states: "Social workers respect and promote the right of clients to self-determination and assist clients in their efforts to identify and clarify their goals. Social workers may limit clients' right to self-determination when, in the social workers' professional judgment, clients' actions or potential actions pose a serious, foreseeable, and imminent risk to themselves or others" (NASW, 2010).

Self-determination means that the social worker and client (individual, couple, family, or group) develop a mutual relationship by which they search for solutions to the client's problem in the interest of promoting growth. In this regard, social workers serve as enablers of change in that they help clients to candidly look at their problems, consider a range of solutions and their potential consequences, and implement strategies that will move them toward healthy functioning. Immanuel Kant (Dolgoff, Loewenberg, & Harrington, 2000, p. 114), an early modern philosopher, stated that a person's right to determine his or her own destiny is an unconditional right. Based on the United States Constitution, self-determination is protected by the Ninth and Fourteenth Amendments. Supreme Court Justice Brandeis suggested that this fundamental right is "the right to be left alone." Social work has always focused on the clients' assumption of responsibility in determining their participation in treatment (Brandeis & Warren, 1890, p. 1).

Informed Consent

This commitment to clients means that social workers must use "clear and understandable language" to inform clients of the purpose of the services, risks related to the services, limits to services because of the requirements of a third-party payer, relevant costs, reasonable alternatives, clients' rights to refuse or withdraw consent, and the time frame covered by the consent. Social workers should also allow clients the opportunity to ask questions about the treatment process and the time frame (NASW, 2010).

Informed consent means that a social worker will not release confidential information about a client unless the client has consented. The problem occurs when another agency needs information on the client based on the client's experience at another agency. Typically, social work agencies require the client's written consent before they will release information. To avoid a delay in securing information, some agencies routinely ask clients to sign a release form at intake that will allow the agency to secure information from previous agencies the client has had contact with. In these instances, social workers should be very clear to ensure that the client understands what signing the consent form means. The form should be readable and specific. If a client is not capable or is too young to provide informed consent, permission should be sought from an appropriate third party.

Professional Boundaries

Professional boundaries mean that there are clear lines of differences that are maintained between the social worker and the client in the interest of preserving the working relationship. The boundary between social worker and client helps to ensure that the relationship is professional and not social. The professional boundary ensures that clients can focus on the concerns for which they are seeking help.

Confidentiality

Confidentiality is essential in the helping process since it entails the revelation of very personal and often painful parts of a client's life. Social workers must adhere to the NASW Code of Ethics to ensure and safeguard client confidentiality.

Sometimes social workers are faced with difficult decisions that present ethical dilemmas for them. Social workers must adhere to the NASW Code of Ethics in dealing with ethical dilemmas. You, as first-year social work students, must talk with your supervisors when presented with an ethical dilemma to ensure that you are being ethically responsible and adhering to the NASW Code of Ethics and agency policies and procedures.

Confidentiality protects the client's well-being. Social workers who violate client confidentiality can cause serious harm to the helping relationship. Typically, social workers cannot reveal or disclose information about clients unless they have first received written permission from the client. Exceptions vary from state to state, but generally include the following:

1. If the client poses a danger to him- or herself or others.
2. If the client waives rights to privilege.
3. If the social worker suspects abuse or neglect of a minor, an elderly or disabled person, or a resident of an institution.

4. If the court orders the social worker to make records available.
5. If the client waives confidentiality when there is a lawsuit.
6. If the client is involved in a legal action and the courts require release of the records.
7. If an emergency exists. (Corey, Corey, & Callanan, 2011; Vanquez, 1993)

Making an ethical decision is a process that occurs over time and results in a person acting in a particular way. It is a process that one gradually moves through by way of a series of steps. A model for ethical decision making as defined by Dolgoff, Loewenberg, & Harrington (2009) is as follows:

Step 1 Identify the problem and the factors that contribute to its maintenance.

Step 2 Identify all of the persons and institutions involved in this problem, such as clients, victims, support systems, other professionals, and others.

Step 3 Determine who should be involved in the decision making.

Step 4 Identify the values relevant to this problem held by the several participants identified in Step 2, including the client's and social worker's personal values, as well as relevant professional, group, and societal values.

Step 5 Identify the goals and objectives whose attainment you believe may resolve (or at least reduce) the problem.

Step 6 Identify alternate intervention strategies and targets.

Step 7 Assess the effectiveness and efficiency of each alternative in terms of the identified goals.

Step 8 Select the most appropriate strategy.

Step 9 Implement the strategy selected.

Step 10 Monitor the implementation, paying particular attention to unanticipated consequences.

Step 11 Evaluate the results and identify additional problems.

UNDERSTANDING OF KNOWLEDGE

Please choose the *best* answer from among the possible choices.

1. Ethics can be defined as:

   a. Values
   b. Moralities
   c. Personal ideas
   d. What is right and correct

2. Values are:

   a. Concerned with "what is good and desirable"
   b. One's personal viewpoints
   c. What social workers think and feel
   d. What all professions think and feel

3. The Code of Ethics defines the ethical responsibilities social workers have to:

   a. Family settings, sibling relationships, and sports organizations
   b. Clients, colleagues, practice settings, and the profession
   c. Political, financial, and social groups and organizations
   d. Churches, sororities, fraternities, and civic organizations

4. All of the following are key ethical principles, except:

   a. Self-determination
   b. Informed consent
   c. Agency procedures
   d. Confidentiality

5. An ethical principle that provides clear lines of differences that are maintained between the social worker and the client in the interest of preserving the working relationship is best known as:

   a. Privacy and confidentiality
   b. Physical contact
   c. Competence
   d. Professional boundary

6. Self-determination is all of the following except:

   a. Protected by the Ninth and Fourteenth Amendments
   b. A key principle of social work
   c. Recognized by Immanuel Kant, an early philosopher
   d. Determined by each individual social worker

7. Informed consent means all of the following except:

   a. A social worker will not release confidential information about a client unless the client has consented.
   b. A parent or caregiver will sign the consent for a child under age 18.
   c. A client will typically be notified at the initial interview about the agency's policy.
   d. Clients have signed a consent form at another agency.

8. Social justice means that social workers will pursue and promote:

   a. Fair and equitable treatment for all persons including people of color and other vulnerable populations
   b. Employment opportunities for disgruntled factory workers who are members of a union
   c. Child abuse prevention and maltreatment
   d. All welfare mothers living in public housing being allowed to attend private colleges without paying tuition

9. An ethical principle in which the social worker shares with the client the purpose of the services, risks related to the services, and limits to services because of the requirements of a third-party payer, is best supporting the principle of:

   a. Confidentiality
   b. Informed consent
   c. Competence
   d. Self-determination

10. A social worker who advocates for a client does so to:

    a. Receive public approval.
    b. Add to his or her achievements.
    c. Assist clients in receiving needed services.
    d. Gain the approval of his/her agency.

11. The Code of Ethics defines the ethical responsibilities social workers have to all of the following except:

    a. To their clients and colleagues
    b. To their universities and colleges
    c. To practice settings and themselves as professionals
    d. To the profession and the broader society

12. An ethical principle of the social work profession which recognizes the right and need of clients to make their own choices and decisions is best known as:

    a. Confidentiality
    b. Competence
    c. Self-determination
    d. Informed consent

13. All are models for ethical decision making as defined by Dolgoff (2009) except:

    a. Identify the problem and the factors that contribute to its maintenance.
    b. Identify the goals and objectives you believe may resolve or reduce the problem.
    c. Select the least appropriate strategy.
    d. Determine who should be involved in the decision making.

14. Social workers cannot reveal or disclose information about clients unless they have first received written permission from the client. Exceptions vary from state to state, but generally include all the following except:

    a. If the client poses a danger to him- or herself or others
    b. If the social worker suspects abuse or neglect of a minor, an elderly or disabled person, or a resident of an institution
    c. If the client waives confidentiality when there is a lawsuit
    d. If the client's spouse requests information

15. When a social worker pursues and promotes fair and equitable treatment for all persons including people of color and other vulnerable populations, he or she is demonstrating the Code of Ethics key ethical responsibility of:

    a. Privacy and confidentiality
    b. Social justice
    c. Self-determination
    d. Cultural competence

MASTERY AND ASSESSMENT OF KNOWLEDGE OF SKILLS

Please choose the *best* answer from among the possible choices.

1. A social worker is faced with a practice situation that poses an ethical dilemma. Who should the social worker contact first?

    a. Social work licensure board for the state
    b. Supervisor
    c. National Association of Social Workers
    d. Counsel on Social Work Education

2. A social worker wishes to video two client sessions. The social worker should get written consent from:

    a. The agency director   c. A coworker
    b. His or her supervisor   d. The client

3. A female social worker provided therapy to a twenty-five-year-old mother over the course of a year. Two years later, another agency that is seeing the mother requests information about her prior treatment without the mother's written consent. The first social worker should:

    a. Deny the request because of the absence of written consent by the mother.
    b. Provide the information without the mother's written consent.
    c. Provide the information based on the mother's verbal consent via phone.
    d. Provide the information after consulting with her supervisor.

4. A social worker is providing therapy to a husband whose wife is not in treatment. The wife inquires of the social worker whether her husband is discussing their marital difficulties. The social worker should respond by:

    a. Probing the wife's reasons for asking for this information.
    b. Sharing that the treatment relationship is confidential and any information would have to come from her husband.
    c. Asking the wife if there are any specific concerns that she has.
    d. Saying to the wife that she is to blame for her husband's problems.

5. A social worker is at a cocktail party that is attended by one of her clients' neighbors. The neighbor wants to know if the social worker is providing help to the client because of his alcohol problems. The social worker should:

    a. Explain that she is providing help to her neighbor for his alcoholism.
    b. Explain to the neighbor that it is not appropriate to discuss with her any client that she is seeing.
    c. Say to the neighbor that she is seeing the client but not for his alcoholism, and question the neighbor about the client's alcoholism.
    d. Ask the neighbor about the client's wife and whether the wife is also an alcoholic.

6. In working with a mentally disabled client, age 26, whose mental capacity is that of a six-year-old, which principle of social work might the social worker give less consideration to?

    a. Respect for the individual
    b. Integrity
    c. Self-determination
    d. Dignity and worth of the individual

7. A first-year social work intern is overheard by her supervisor telling a client that she would like to participate with her in a political rally for a political candidate that they both endorse. The supervisor should:

   a. Invite the intern into her office and explain that it's not appropriate to engage clients in this manner, and discuss the issue of boundaries.
   b. Invite the intern into her office and engage her in a discussion about the political candidate.
   c. Say nothing to the intern.
   d. Terminate the intern based on this observation.

8. A social worker is providing therapy to three clients, all of whom are friends. The social worker is told by two of the clients that the third client has been saying negative things about her. Which step should the social worker follow?

   a. Confront the third client about what she has heard.
   b. Tell the third client that she can no longer work with her because of the hearsay.
   c. Discuss with each of the three clients that they are free to discuss anything among themselves, including issues pertaining to her. However, any comments made about her cannot be brought into the treatment process to avoid mistrust.
   d. Discuss issues addressed in treatment by the third client with the two other clients.

9. A teacher tells a school social worker that a mother the social worker is seeing as a client is involved in an intimate relationship with the husband of another one of her clients. The social worker should:

   a. Encourage the discussion with the teacher to elicit more information.
   b. Ignore the teacher and walk away.
   c. Say to the teacher that it is not professionally appropriate for her to engage in conversation with any teacher about any of her clients.
   d. Inform the teacher that she is a "gossip."

10. A minister of a local church refers a young mother who is experiencing marital difficulties to a family service agency. He specifically asks the mother to request a social worker who attends his church, because she is an excellent therapist. The minister later asks the social worker to detail information about the mother's treatment and whether the mother has discussed the issue of domestic violence. The social worker should:

    a. Engage the minister in discussing the client's issues.
    b. Engage the minister about the client's relationship with the married man who is a member of the church.

    c. Tell the minister that referrals are appreciated; however, she is not at liberty to discuss anything about the client without the client's written consent.

    d. Tell the minister that she would prefer to discuss these issues with the minister's wife, with whom she is friendly.

11. A client is completing an intake interview with a social worker and requests that she be seen by a worker who utilizes cognitive behavioral therapy (CBT). The social worker uses psychodynamic theory and has very limited knowledge of CBT. The intake social worker should:

    a. See the client herself utilizing the psychodynamic perspective.

    b. Refer the client to the agency social worker who is very well versed in CBT.

    c. Inform the client that she doesn't support the use of CBT and encourage the client to see her or another worker who use the psychodynamic framework.

    d. Tell the client that she is not in a position to request a specific type of treatment.

12. A male social worker employed at a family agency for three years admits to his supervisor that he had sex with a client. In this case, the supervisor should:

    a. Report the social worker to the licensure board for the state and give the client's name so that the case can be reviewed.

    b. Immediately discuss with the social worker that having sex with the client is wrong.

    c. Report the social worker to the licensure board for the state without providing the client's name so that the case can be reviewed.

    d. Consult with the client before taking actions to determine if the sex was consensual.

13. A 26-year-old social worker is providing therapy to a 25-year-old client. During the initial session the social worker learns that their backgrounds are similar. At the end of the session, the client invites the social worker to a party at her home as a means of appreciation and states that she would "fit in" with her friends. The social worker should:

    a. Thank the client and accept the invitation.

    b. Explain to the client that their relationship must be professional and cannot become a friendship.

    c. Ask the client for the names of her friends.

    d. Inform the client that she must first consult with her supervisor.

14. A male social worker has been assigned to provide therapy to a female who he dated and with whom he had an intimate relationship a year and a half ago. The male social worker should:

   a. Agree to provide therapy to the female, since their relationship was a year and a half ago.
   b. Provide therapy and not mention the earlier dating relationship.
   c. State that it is unethical for him to provide therapy to the female and refer her to another social worker.
   d. Provide therapy and engage the female in denying the former relationship to anyone at the agency.

15. A male social worker employed by a family agency is counseling a female client for her depression. The agency has a sliding scale fee. The client asks the social worker to say that her salary is less than what it actually is so that her fee can be $20 per session rather than the $90 per session based on her actual salary. The social worker should:

   a. Tell the client that it is not professionally ethical for him to say her salary is less than it actually is.
   b. Agree with the client to the lesser salary so that she pays the $20 per session.
   c. Terminate the client for making such a suggestion.
   d. Accept the client's suggestion of the lower fee if the client agrees to share the $70 difference per session with him.

16. A married male supervisor develops an intimate relationship with a second-year female MSW intern at the agency in which she is placed. The statement that best reflects the ethical principle that should determine the supervisor's response is:

   a. The behavior is acceptable if the supervisor and intern keep the relationship quiet during agency hours.
   b. The behavior is acceptable if the agency director is informed.
   c. The behavior is acceptable if the supervisor and social work intern agree to the relationship.
   d. The behavior is unethical and violates the NASW Code of Ethics given the power imbalance that exists between supervisor and supervisee.

17. A client's insurance company asks a social worker to fax a client's record to the insurance company to enable the insurance company to determine if the client's treatment should be reimbursed. The social worker should:

   a. Send the client's record.
   b. Mail the record rather than fax it.
   c. Refuse the request.
   d. Seek the client's written permission before revealing any information.

18. A client calls her former social worker to seek her assistance. The client is now addicted to crack and is showing withdrawal symptoms including vomiting and sweating. The former social worker should:

   a. Give the former client an immediate appointment to see her.
   b. Have the former client call her neighbor.
   c. Immediately secure medical help for the client.
   d. Tell the client to drink some water and a take nap.

19. A social worker employed by a family service agency notices that a member of her sorority is in the waiting room. The social worker should:

   a. Greet the sorority member and inquire why she is there.
   b. Ignore the sorority member's presence in the waiting room.
   c. Greet the sorority member and not engage in any conversation.
   d. Greet the sorority member and invite her into her office to talk with her before her appointment.

20. A six-month-old infant was kept in the hospital due to withdrawal from drugs because of his drug-addicted mother. A foster home has been located for the infant because the mother's whereabouts are unknown. The social worker should:

   a. Tell the foster parents that the infant is healthy and should have no problems.
   b. Tell the foster parents that the mother was on drugs, but that the child has shown no signs of being impacted by the drugs.
   c. Tell the foster parents that the infant's mother was addicted to drugs, that the child has evidence of withdrawal signs and may have some medical or developmental problems, and that the agency will work with the foster parents to provide support.
   d. Place the child with a foster parent without any discussions about the infant's drug addictions.

21. A fourteen-year-old girl who has been sexually abused by both her natural father and foster father is being placed in another foster home. This is the child's fourth foster home and she is very angry and destructive toward adults, children, and property. The social worker assigned to this case should:

   a. Not tell the new foster parents about the child's early history, including the sexual abuse.
   b. Tell the new foster parents that the child has been in three other foster homes, but has shown no overt problems.
   c. Say nothing to the new foster parents.
   d. Tell the new foster parents about the child's early life experiences including the sexual abuse and that the child is very angry and shows destructive behaviors.

22. A twelve-year-old girl is being seen by a school social worker at a middle school. The twelve-year-old tells the social worker that her father comes into her room each night and has sex with her. The twelve-year-old does not want the social worker to "tell her secret" because she is afraid the father will "kill my mother," as he said he would do if she told the secret to anyone. The social worker should:

    a. Agree with the twelve-year-old that she will keep the secret so that the child is less frightened and fearful.
    b. Call the Department of Family and Children Services without telling the child that she is contacting them and why she is contacting them.
    c. Tell the child that she cannot keep the information secret because it is hurtful to the child and the law requires that the social worker inform adults so the child is not further harmed.
    d. Contact the mother to talk with her about what the child has told her before she contacts the Department of Family and Children Services.

23. A violation of ethical conduct with a mother may exist when a social worker:

    a. Discusses the child's early developmental history.
    b. Discusses the child's school performance.
    c. Discusses her (the social worker's) challenges with her child.
    d. Discusses the child's participation in after-school activities.

Reflective Essay Questions

1. What ethical dilemma(s) have you as a student faced at your agency? How was the ethical dilemma handled? Did you agree or disagree with how the ethical dilemma was handled? Why?

2. Give an example where you have unconsciously violated a client's autonomy (right to self-determination) or confidentiality and privacy, or have witnessed or discussed such a situation while at your field placement agency. Discuss the knowledge you gained from those exchanges.

3. Discuss at least two ethical principles in the NASW Code of Ethics that you most strongly support, and why.

4. Identify and discuss particular issues and concerns that are not addressed by the NASW Code of Ethics but you feel should be included, and why.

5. Identify and discuss two policies that you are familiar with in your MSW program and at your agency that, to some degree, lack some clarity in support of the NASW Code of Ethics. Discuss how you would either amend or perform a total overhaul of the policy.

3

CRITICAL
THINKING

DETAILED UNDERSTANDING
AND EXPLANATION (DUE)

Many professions utilize critical thinking as a tool for decision making; however, no profession has benefited from its practice more than the helping professions. The history of the mental health professions (psychology, psychiatry, counseling, human services, and social work) is replete with the application of critical thinking as a practice tool when working with social problems and troubled clients (Addis & Krasnow, 2000; Baer, 2003; Busfield, 2001; and Baron & Sternberg, 1993). Brookfield (1995) defines critical thinking as a "unique kind of purposeful thinking in which we use standards such as clarity and fairness that involve the careful examination and evaluation of beliefs and actions in order to arrive at well-reasoned decisions." It is thinking that is clear, precise, specific, and accurate. It is thoughts that are relevant to the problem, consistent to the situation, significant and not trivial as well as fair versus biased or one-sided (Paul, 1993). Kirst-Ashman defines critical thinking as: "(1) the careful scrutiny of what is stated as true or what appears to be true and the resulting expression of an opinion or conclusion based on that scrutiny, and (2) the creative formulation of an opinion or conclusion when presented with a question, problem, or issue" (2007, p. 7).

Critical thinking in social work is essential because it requires that you, as social work students, must learn to question theories and assumptions about people's behaviors and actions. This means you must be willing to ask questions, do an assessment of the issues involved, and develop a conclusion regarding matters with which you are faced. You must be prepared to respond to questions that require that you use critical-thinking skills. Your acceptance into the MSW program was based on your having a liberal arts background in your undergraduate studies. This means that you took courses such as economics, history, English, mathematics, anthropology, sociology, and biology among other courses. These courses will assist you in critically thinking about

social work issues you will be addressing. Your social work training will intro-
duce you to courses in practice, human behavior in the social environment,
policy, and research. As well, you will be required to do a field practicum experience during your first year in the MSW program. You will draw upon your
MSW courses, your field experience, and your undergraduate liberal arts courses in your academic work and in your work with clients. Your ability to pull
from, synthesize, and integrate ideas from all of these sources will require critical thinking on your part.

Your first year instructors will evaluate you, in part, based on your participation in classes. This will mean that you will balance talking and listening,
and apply concepts learned in the classroom with case material discussed in
the classroom and assigned cases in your field experience. Your contributions
to classroom discussions will require self-reflection on your part. Your ability
to be self-reflective will mean that you will learn to understand your own values, prejudices, reasoning skills, and capacity to listen to the viewpoints of others and assess their comments against your own viewpoints. This process will
continually engage your critical-thinking abilities. Once you have been assigned to a field internship, you will be asked to develop a learning contract
with your supervisor that will focus on goals you hope to successfully achieve
over the course of your first field practicum experience. This process will further enhance and enrich your self-reflective critical-thinking skills.

Critical thinking means that you will learn to think for yourself. This will
involve your using related knowledge and skills in everyday life that require
flexibility and a keen interest in discovering mistakes in your thinking, which
will aid you in your final decision-making process. Critical thinkers question
what others view as self-evident (Paul, 1993). Gambrill (2006, p. 15) identified
the following fifteen related skills and knowledge needed for critical thinking:

1. Clarify the problem.
2. Identify significant similarities and differences.
3. Recognize contradictions and inconsistencies.
4. Refine generalizations and avoid oversimplifications.
5. Clarify issues, conclusions, or beliefs.
6. Analyze or evaluate arguments, interpretations, beliefs, or theories.
7. Identify unstated assumptions.
8. Use sound criteria for evaluation.
9. Clarify values and standards.
10. Detect bias and/or prejudice.
11. Distinguish relevant from irrelevant questions, data, claims,
    or reasons.
12. Evaluate your own reasoning process.
13. Make interdisciplinary connections.

14. Analyze and evaluate actions or policies.
15. Evaluate perspectives, interpretations, or theories.

Your critical thinking will be further refined when you learn various treatment theories and the context in which these theories and their application to practice were developed. You will learn to critique theories for any biases they may have as they relate to race, culture, sexual orientation, and class issues so that you can determine which theories are best applied to the diverse client populations you will be discussing in the classroom and seeing in the field. You will learn to evaluate the strengths and weaknesses of various theoretical frameworks during your first year and become adept in learning how to apply various theories to clients. Because you will be taking courses in several sequence areas to include practice, human behavior in the social environment, policy, and research, you will develop critical skills in knowing how to integrate content learned in each of these areas to classroom discussions of clients. You will also be able to apply what you have learned to your actual work with clients during your first field internship. In the various papers you write for your different courses, you will learn to integrate ideas from across the different sequences and draw conclusions based on your ability to synthesize information from these various sources. Because the ideas and theories you will be learning are different, and sometimes seemingly incongruent with each other, you will learn to tolerate and live with a certain degree of uncertainty and ambiguity, which is important for your learning as a first-year student.

In human behavior in the social environment, you will begin to learn how to use the Diagnostic and Statistical Manual of Mental Disorders IV (DSM-IV-TR) published by the American Psychiatric Association. The manual covers all categories of mental health disorders for both adults and children. The updated version, DSM-IV-TR (4th edition text revision) was published in 2000 and contains minor text revisions in the descriptions of each of the 250 mental disorders it lists. The manual is non-theoretical and focuses mostly on describing symptoms as well as statistics concerning which gender is most affected by the illness, the typical age of onset, the effects of treatment, and common treatment approaches. Mental health providers use the manual to better understand a client's potential needs as well as a tool for assessment and diagnosis (APA, 2000).

The DSM-IV-TR has a multiaxial approach that is based on five different dimensions: clinical syndromes, personality and mental retardation, medical condition, psychosocial and environmental problems, and global assessment of functioning. Clinical Syndromes, which is Axis I, describes clinical symptoms that cause significant impairments. These disorders are grouped into different categories, including adjustment disorders, anxiety disorders, and pervasive development disorders. Axis II is Personality and Mental Retardation, which describes long-term problems that are overlooked in the presence of

Axis I disorders. Personality disorders cause significant problems in how a patient relates to the world and include antisocial personality and histrionic personality disorders. Mental retardation is characterized by intellectual impairment and deficits in other areas such as self-care and interpersonal skills (APA, 2000).

The final three categories of the DSM-IV-TR are Axis III, Medical Condition; Axis IV, Psychosocial and Environmental Problems; and Axis V, Global Assessment of Functioning. Axis III includes physical and medical conditions that may influence or worsen Axis I and Axis II disorders such as HIV/AIDS and brain injuries. Axis IV, Psychosocial and Environmental Problems, will be the area about which you will learn the most as a social work student, and where you will become skilled as a social worker and an expert once you become a licensed clinical social worker. Axis IV will help you assess any social or environmental problem that may impact Axis I or Axis II disorders. This may include such factors as unemployment, relocation, the incarceration of a spouse, or the death of a loved one. The Global Assessment of Functioning, Axis V, is the final category of the DSM-IV-TR. This axis will allow you to rate the client's overall level of functioning. Based on this assessment, you will better understand how the other four axes are interacting and the effect on the individual's life (APA, 2000).

In your first-year human behavior in the social environment courses, you will come to understand the DSM-IV-TR diagnostic categories without the need to see people in narrow terms but in their totality, with strengths as well as vulnerabilities. As you come to understand the DSM-IV-TR diagnostic categories, you will begin to use the language used by all mental health professionals. You will come to appreciate and value that people are more complex than any diagnostic category implies. You will learn to engage with clients in a collaborative way so that their capacity for growth is maximized. You will learn that people are resilient and have many ego strengths along with their vulnerabilities, and that understanding their strengths will allow you to empower them in developing areas in which they are vulnerable. You will come to understand that empowerment of clients, whether as individuals or as a family, group, organization, or community, is important for their growth and that your use of empathy and the development of a relationship of trust will be the foundation upon which the client's growth will be promoted. You will learn what is involved in the helping process to include engagement, developing a contract with the client, establishing treatment goals, the various phases of the treatment process (beginning, middle, and end), and successfully terminating your work with a client. As well, you will learn how to refer clients for additional resources when it is indicated and appropriate.

Another aspect of your critical thinking will be your learning not only theories and their application to practice, but, as well, how to evaluate your work with clients. Critical thinking and evidence-based practice go hand in hand and encourage asking questions designed to make the invisible visible. Problems may remain unsolved if you rely on questionable criteria to evaluate claims about what is accurate, such as tradition, popularity, or authority; this was a key reason for the development of evidenced-based practice (Gambrill, 2006).

In your first-year research course(s), you will learn critical-thinking skills that will assist you in evaluating the work you do with your clients from a scientific, systematic approach. You will learn how to describe and carefully appraise your decisions and points of view, logically and systematically, regarding service delivery. This will be done in an effort to arrive at decisions that do more good than harm to your clients. This means that you will pay attention to the process of reasoning (how you think), not just the end result (resolution of problem). Critical thinking and evidenced-based research will encourage you to examine the context in which problems occur, connecting private troubles with public issues to ensure that you are meeting the goals you and the client have established (Dolgoff & Feldstein, 2009).

You will also draw upon research methods that will assist you in evaluating your practice. You will learn about both quantitative and qualitative research and program evaluation and when it is appropriate to draw upon one or all of these methods. Understanding these methods will help you become more effective in your clinical work so that you will be able to measure your effectiveness with clients. As well, you will learn how to structure your social work interventions so that you can evaluate the results to inform future practice. This will help you to know whether you are being maximally helpful to your clients.

There are several philosophical policy perspectives that you will also use in shaping your responses to clients and issues. These philosophical policy areas include conservatism, liberalism, and radicalism. You will need to have a working understanding of each of these philosophical perspectives in order to make responsible decisions with clients. You will also need to draw upon your liberal arts background and the MSW coursework you are learning.

A conservative policy perspective typically implies that individuals are responsible for themselves and that there should be a minimum of government involvement. Three principles characterize the conservative perspective, as follows:

1. Conservatives tend to defend the status quo (the existing state of affairs) and typically are bound by tradition and oppose major proposals for change. In other words, the conservative perspective implies "if something is not broken, don't fix it."
2. They typically view human nature cynically and their view of people is that they are self-interested, corrupt, and lazy. For example, conservatives abhor people on welfare because they believe welfare recipients are taking from society and not contributing to it—that people

on welfare do not deserve to be on any form of assistance and should secure jobs that will enable them to take care of themselves and their children. They believe that hard work, ambition, and self-reliance will result in success.

3. They desire little, if any, government involvement. They believe that individual effort, tax reductions, and free economy will best achieve social welfare. Conservatives generally encourage individual achievement and favor the expansion of the private sector (Dolgoff, 2010).

A liberal perspective suggests that it is important for government to be involved in the social, political, and economic structures. Liberals further believe that it is the role of government to protect all peoples' rights and privileges. Hence, government should be involved in the social, political, and economic structures established by the government. Dolgoff and Feldstein (2009) identify three principles that characterize the liberal perspective:

1. Liberals believe in equity before the law and equal treatment by the state.
2. They uphold the protection of individual rights and freedoms as major civil liberties and constitutional rights and privileges.
3. Liberals view the government as a necessary protector of individuals from abuse by the market and social forces. They disfavor legal enforcement of morality.

Persons who believe in radicalism take the extreme view that fundamental change is essential if this country is to be fair and truly responsive to social and economic justice for all. Those with radical perspectives see poverty as caused by the exploitation of the poor by the rich (Karger and Stoesz, 2002, pp. 115–116). Radicals state that the rich pay low wages to maintain their wealth and to keep poor people poor and in the lower class of society. If poor people complain, radicals feel that they will be fired since there are many other poor people to take their place.

You, as social work students, must draw upon these philosophical perspectives—in addition to liberal arts courses taken as undergraduates and the theories you are exposed to in the MSW program—to respond to your clients and the issues they bring. During your first year, in addition to policy perspectives, you will draw upon the various theories to which you will be exposed in human behavior and the social environment and practice, to include the ecological perspective and strengths perspective. You will learn how to use these perspectives in your work with individuals, families, groups, organizations, and communities.

As social work students, you will become well informed about the principles and guidelines that support reasoned judgment. You will integrate the use of sound insightful understanding of practice theories in your classroom discussions about cases and in your work with clients in the field. You will utilize the critical-thinking skills learned from your course work and field practice experiences. You will be able to draw upon what you learned in your policy courses to advocate for policy and legislation that support the needs of your clients. You will adopt logical investigative techniques from your research class assignments as well as from your field practicum observations and experiences. Your actions will be augmented by your creativity along with your curiosity in your work with clients. Lastly, you will demonstrate the ability as a first-year student to use critical thinking in the classroom and in the field as you complete the foundation year and move to the advanced specialization year.

UNDERSTANDING OF KNOWLEDGE

Please choose the *best* answer from among the possible choices.

1. In the mental health professions, critical thinking is used in:

   a. Psychology and psychiatry
   b. Counseling
   c. Human services and social work
   d. All of the above

2. Critical thinking for MSW students draws upon all of the following *except*:

   a. Liberal arts background
   b. Opinions of others
   c. MSW courses
   d. Field practicum

3. Skills and knowledge needed for critical thinking include all of the following *except*:

   a. Clarify the problem.
   b. Detect bias and/or prejudice.
   c. Absence of cultural competence
   d. Make interdisciplinary connections.

4. Critical thinking is thinking that is:

   a. Clear, precise, specific, and accurate
   b. Long-winded and general
   c. Unfocused and spotty
   d. Unstructured sentences and paragraphs

5. The DSM-IV-TR is used by:

   a. Social workers only
   b. Psychiatrists only
   c. All mental health professionals
   d. Psychologists only

6. The acronym DSM-IV-TR means:

   a. Diagnostic Student Manual
   b. Developmental Systems Method
   c. Diagnostic and Statistical Manual
   d. Drug Substance Management

7. An area of the DSM-IV-TR in which social workers are the most skilled is:

   a. Axis I, which describes clinical symptoms that cause significant impairments
   b. Axis II, which focuses on personality and mental retardation
   c. Axis III, which focuses on medical conditions
   d. Axis IV, which focuses on psychosocial and environmental problems

8. Evidenced-based practice means that you:

   a. Will evaluate the work you do with your clients from a scientific, systematic approach.
   b. Will evaluate your agency and its practices.
   c. Will evaluate agency administration including your supervisor.
   d. Will evaluate agency colleagues.

9. The policy perspective that tends to defend the status quo (the existing state of affairs), is typically bound by tradition, and opposes major proposals for change is best known as:

   a. Conservative
   b. Radical
   c. Liberal
   d. Independent

10. The policy perspective that suggests that government should be involved in the social, political, and economic structures established by the government is:

    a. Tea Party
    b. Radical
    c. Liberal
    d. Independent

11. A radical policy perspective states that:

   a. People are self-interested, corrupt, and lazy.
   b. Fundamental change is essential if this country is to be fair and truly responsive to social and economic justice for all.
   c. Government should be involved in the social, political, and economic structures established by the government.
   d. People enjoy fighting for their own rights.

12. First-year students learn generalist practice, which means that they work with:

   a. Individuals, families, groups, organizations, and communities
   b. Child welfare clients only
   c. Criminally insane clients only
   d. Homeless population only

13. MSW students take courses in the following areas:

   a. Religion, human behavior in the social environment, economics, and business
   b. Practice, human behavior in the social environment, research, and policy
   c. Sociology, criminal justice, biology, and practice
   d. Research, history, anthropology, and Spanish

14. MSW students typically come to social work with an academic background in:

   a. Business
   b. Nursing
   c. Liberal arts
   d. Accounting

15. A major critical-thinking quality an MSW student must have is the capacity for:

   a. Sympathy
   b. Self-interest
   c. Self-centeredness
   d. Self-reflection

MASTERY AND ASSESSMENT OF KNOWLEDGE OF SKILLS

Please choose the *best* answer from among the possible choices.

Questions 1 to 10 are based on the following paragraph:

Virginia has weekly psychoeducational group sessions with her five clients (Paul, Robert, Alice, Ruth, and Susan) focused on employment seeking, which includes skills such as finding a job, dressing appropriately for an interview and for a job, as well as writing a résumé. Prior to one of the sessions, her immediate supervisor, Ms. Smith, came into the room before the group started. She asked Virginia what her psychoeducational group was focusing on. Virginia explained that the psychoeducational group was focused on finding a job. Ms. Smith leaned toward Virginia's ear and whispered, in audible terms, "Do you think anybody will hire these stupid idiots? One is a homo and the others are losers." Virginia was shocked as Ms. Smith laughed and left the room. Suddenly the room was silent and it was obvious that members of the group had overheard Ms. Smith's comments.

1.   What steps should Virginia take?

   a.   Go and get her supervisor, Ms. Smith, and insist that she apologize to the group members about her comments because it is clear that the group overheard Ms. Smith's comments.
   b.   Do nothing and proceed to conduct the psychoeducational group focused on finding a job as planned.
   c.   Apologize to the group about Ms. Smith's inappropriate and insensitive behavior, tell members that the agency will be informed and appropriate action taken, and address the group about their feelings regarding Ms. Smith's statement.
   d.   Immediately leave the room and go look for the director, Ms. Florida, to inform her of what has happened and bring her back to talk with the group.

2.   When Virginia speaks with Ms. Smith, she should address all of the following *except*:

   a.   She should remind her that her professional behavior.
   b.   That she must be in accord with the ethics and values of the profession.
   c.   That her comment was spoken too loudly and that she should have texted her instead of whispering in audible terms.
   d.   That she must address this matter with the director.

3. If Virginia did nothing in response to Ms. Smith's comment, all of the following could have happened *except*:

   a. Her nonresponsiveness would lessen the trust by members toward both Virginia and Ms. Smith.
   b. Paul, Robert, Alice, Ruth, and Susan would be puzzled, frustrated, and disappointed.
   c. Paul, Robert, Alice, Ruth, and Susan would feel disrespected by members of the agency staff.
   d. Paul, Robert, Alice, Ruth, and Susan would just pretend that it never happened.

4. The following actions are appropriate for Virginia to take immediately following Ms. Smith's remarks with the exception of:

   a. Apologizing to the group about Ms. Smith's behavior and its inappropriateness.
   b. Asking the group members to discuss their feelings regarding what they just experienced.
   c. Misleading the group to believe that they misunderstood what Ms. Smith said.
   d. Assisting the group members in understanding that what Ms. Smith said does not represent the agency or the profession.

5. Virginia speaks with her supervisor, Ms. Smith, as was advised by her faculty field advisor. It is awkward for Virginia because she is a student who has to talk with her supervisor to inform her that her group members were upset with the supervisor's comments. Ms. Smith apologizes to Virginia and agrees that Virginia should discuss the matter with the director. The director should:

   a. Say to Virginia and Ms. Smith that the matter has been handled by Virginia and no further action is needed.
   b. Tell Virginia that as a student, she should not have talked with her faculty field advisor and that she has overstepped her authority.
   c. Tell Virginia that she will talk with her faculty field advisor and her supervisor, Ms. Smith, about the matter.
   d. Thank Virginia for having talked with the group; speak individually with Ms. Smith, the supervisor; speak with the faculty field advisor; and arrange several agency meetings focused on diversity and cultural sensitivity.

6. Virginia should contact her faculty field advisor:

   a. Immediately after Ms. Smith's comment
   b. Immediately after a discussion with the group about what they experienced
   c. After she has spoken with the director
   d. At the next field seminar meeting in two weeks

7. Virginia should contact her faculty field advisor for all of the following reasons *except*:

   a. To ensure that the steps she took were appropriate.
   b. To confirm that her plans to talk with her supervisor are appropriate.
   c. To validate that her plans to speak with the director are appropriate.
   d. To laugh with him about Ms. Smith's comment.

8. When Virginia speaks with her faculty field advisor regarding the NASW Codes that Ms. Smith violated, he will address all of the following *except*:

   a. The NASW Code of Ethics 1.01 – Commitment to Clients, which states, "Social workers' primary responsibility is to promote the well-being of clients. . . . clients' interests are primary."
   b. The NASW Code of Ethics 3.03 – Performance Evaluation, which states, "Social workers who have responsibility for evaluating the performance of others should fulfill such responsibility in a fair and considerate manner and on the basis of clearly stated criteria."
   c. The NASW Code of Ethics 1.05 – Cultural Competence and Social Diversity, which states, "Social workers should obtain education about and seek to understand the nature of social diversity and oppression with respect to race, ethnicity, national origin, color, sex, sexual orientation, gender identity or expression, age, marital status, political belief, religion, immigration, status and mental or physical disability."
   d. The NASW Code of Ethics 1.12 – Derogatory Language, which states, "Social workers should not use derogatory language in their written or verbal communications to or about clients."

9. As a social worker, Ms. Smith must function in accord with the values, ethics, and standards set forth for social workers and must be reminded of the following standards with the exception of:

   a. Standard 7 – Diverse Workforce, which states, "Social workers shall support and advocate for recruitment, admissions and hiring, and retention efforts in social work programs and agencies that ensure diversity within the profession."

    b. Standard 2 – Self-Awareness, which states, "Social workers shall seek to develop an understanding of their own personal, cultural values and beliefs as one way of appreciating the importance of multicultural identities in the lives of people."

    c. Standard 3 – Cross-Cultural Knowledge, which states, "Social workers shall have and continue to develop specialized knowledge and understanding about the history, traditions, values, family systems, and artistic expressions of major client groups that they serve."

    d. Standard 4 – Cross-Cultural Skills, which states, "Social workers shall use appropriate methodological approaches, skills, and techniques that reflect the workers' understanding of the role of culture in the helping process."

10. Which is the best response regarding the psychological affect Virginia's immediately leaving the room after Ms. Smith's comment would have on the group members?

    a. It would leave them alone, fearful and unclear about what had just transpired.

    b. It would leave them without information regarding locating employment.

    c. It would leave them without information on writing a résumé.

    d. It would leave them without information regarding how to dress appropriately for a job interview.

Questions 11 to 12 are based on the following paragraph:

Robert is a 19-year-old Caucasian who has openly stated that he is gay and has been in two foster homes since the age of 12. His father died of AIDS when he was 10 and his mother subsequently died of complications from AIDS when he was 13. No relatives wanted Robert because of the stigma associated with AIDS, although Robert did not have HIV or AIDS. Robert was, however, gay, and publicly identified as such. Robert's high school grades were good and his behavior was within an acceptable range, with occasional fighting with peers because of his gay lifestyle. He had been in two foster homes and was removed from his first foster home because his foster mother became ill with cancer and could no longer keep him. Robert had a close relationship with the foster mother and it was clear that she loved Robert and Robert loved her. He did well with his second foster parents and is now in the MTM because he has aged out of foster care.

11. In your initial meeting with Robert, he tells you that he prefers to have a gay social worker. You should:

    a. Respect his wishes and refer him to at least two qualified gay social workers in your unit.
    b. Ask Robert why he would prefer to see a gay social worker.
    c. Explain to Robert that you are bisexual and ask him if that counts.
    d. Reassure Robert that you have worked with other gay clients and are willing to learn more about homosexuality.

12. Robert is so grateful and appreciative for all the help that he received from MTM that he decides to pursue a degree in social work. He is accepted into a BSW program and graduates and then into an MSW program from which he graduates. Robert secures a job at the local welfare office, does well, and is promoted to supervisor over his unit. Pleased with his performance, Robert recommends a friend for a supervisory position. He later learns that the agency's personnel officer has been diverting job applications from gay and lesbian applicants with the tacit approval of the agency director. As a result, Robert's friend, who is openly gay, is not considered for employment, though perhaps qualified. What ethical principles drawn from the social work Code of Ethics should guide Robert's actions in this situation?

    a. Robert should take aggressive professional action to end the discrimination.
    b. Robert should explore his own values and act accordingly.
    c. Robert should resign from the agency both as a protest and because the agency is behaving unethically.
    d. Robert should call his friend and suggest that he contact the media.

13. In a family counseling setting, a family is referred in which a child is living with his mother and stepfather. The child has expressed a desire to live with his biological father. In this situation, the social worker should hold the first interview with:

    a. The mother and stepfather
    b. The mother, stepfather, and child
    c. The mother and natural father
    d. The mother and child

14. A client, in a session with you at your agency, indicates he is suicidal, has a gun, and intends to kill himself that day. You should call:

    a. The nearest hospital
    b. A social agency
    c. The police
    d. His family

15. When an elderly person enters a nursing home, there is a period of adjustment. Some residents characteristically withdraw, while others are more talkative. When a client withdraws in the first weeks of residence, the social worker's first task is usually to:

    a. Discuss the resident's hesitation about participation in activities.
    b. Encourage the family to visit more often.
    c. Help the person become involved with programs and activities.
    d. Encourage staff to draw the person into floor routines.

Reflective Essay Questions

1. Discuss your understanding of the critical thinking process and its relevance to inform and communicate professional judgment as a first-year social work student both in the classroom and at your field placement.

2. Discuss the sources (political, social, and economic factors) of influence that you have observed, been part of, or have heard about at your agency that have had an effect on the way in which clinical decisions are made and critical thinking is processed.

3. As critical thinking is not just thinking, but thinking which entails self-improvement, discuss the ways in which your judgment, problem solving, and decision making has improved since your understanding of the application of critical thinking to your learning and practice of social work.

4. Making choices and predictions in which personal obstacles interfere is routine for any master-level program, but particularly for the social work profession. Discuss ways in which some individual barriers have interfered with your developing and using critical-thinking skills.

5. To practice the process of critical thinking, discuss the purpose of this chapter on critical thinking, what the author is trying to accomplish, and your understanding of the concepts that are important to you. Be as succinct and concise as possible. Also, try this exercise with a classroom lecture in your MSW program or an in-service training at your field placement.

4

DIVERSITY IN PRACTICE

DETAILED UNDERSTANDING
AND EXPLANATION (DUE)

The United States is undergoing major demographic shifts so that we are seeing the "browning" and "aging" of America. The 1990s and 2000s have witnessed a large population growth with significant increases in people of color, particularly Latinos. These changes will result in a more diverse population that will confront you in your future work with clients. As well, this increase in diversity will impact your social work practice, which will require that you are culturally sensitive and culturally competent.

Diversity is not an idea that should be an "add-on" to the social work curriculum, but should be integrated throughout the social work courses that you will be taught. Understanding diversity is key to your being able to work with people across a spectrum of client populations. Your ability to work with diverse clients will intersect well with your focus on social justice, another core competency of social work. Diversity and social justice are especially important for assisting people who are marginalized, oppressed, and in poverty.

The National Association of Social Workers Code of Ethics (2008) and Indicators for the Achievement of the NASW Standards for Cultural Competence in Social Work (2001) specifically state that it is not ethical to practice without the knowledge, skills, and expertise needed to provide culturally relevant services in an increasingly diverse world. Four standards especially important for you to fully understand and appreciate are as follows:

- Standard 2 – Self-Awareness: "Social workers shall seek to develop their own personal, cultural values and beliefs as one way of appreciating the importance of multicultural identities in the lives of people."
- Standard 3 – Cross-Cultural Knowledge: "Social workers shall have and continue to develop specialized knowledge and understanding

about the history, traditions, values, family systems, and artistic expressions of major client groups that they serve."

- Standard 4 – Cross-Cultural Skills: "Social workers shall use appropriate methodological approaches, skills, and techniques that reflect the workers' understanding of the role of culture in the helping process."
- Standard 9 – Language Diversity: "Social workers shall seek to provide or advocate for the provision of information, referrals, and services in the language appropriate for the client, which may include use of interpreters."

You will be educated to understand the dynamics of oppression, how oppression impacts certain individuals and groups in this country, and how you can work to lessen oppression and promote social and economic justice. Oppression is "the systematic, institutionalized mistreatment of one group of people by another for whatever reason" (Yamato, 1993, p. 207). Usually, persons in power are able to overtly and covertly oppress groups that have little or no power. In the United States, the federal government defines four groups that experience oppression requiring affirmative action laws that protect them. These four groups are: African Americans or Blacks, Hispanics or Latinos, Native Americans, and Asian Americans/Pacific Islanders. From 1990 to 2000 the total population in the United States increased from 248.7 million to 281.4 million, with an increase in the ethnic minority population from 60 million to 86.9 million—a 44.83% increase. By the year 2050 Whites alone will make up 72.1% of the population; Blacks alone will make up 14.6%; Asians alone will make up 8.0%; Hispanics will make up 24.4%; Whites alone not Hispanic will make up 50.1% (U.S. Census, 2010). These statistics show that the United States is "browning" at a rapid pace, and your work will require that you are culturally competent.

Listed below are very brief summary statements on each of the four ethnic minority groups in this country that you are likely to have contact with. It is important to note that the facts stated are general and that it will be important for you to make your assessments and interventions based on a comprehensive psychosocial evaluation of each individual client and his or her family. The information below serves as a guide, but in no way takes the place of your individual work with the client that you will be seeing and the information the client will provide to you during the intake process and over the course of treatment. Your clients are your first sources of knowledge and what they tell you about their families is critical to your assessment and intervention strategies. Each client is unique and no two clients can be seen as identical to the other.

African Americans or Blacks

African Americans entered the United States as slaves and although they were emancipated under President Abraham Lincoln, following the Civil War, oppression and discrimination were rampant throughout the United States, but particularly in the South. The Civil Rights Act of 1964 under President Lyndon B. Johnson brought many changes for African Americans in the areas of employment, transportation, and education. History shows the struggles, hardships, and difficulties faced by African Americans up to and including the Civil Rights movement headed by Dr. Martin Luther King, Jr. The election of an African American president, Barack Obama, in 2008, represented a major victory not only for African Americans but for this country. While this election was seen as historic and as representing a breakthrough in race relations in this country, some degree of racism and discrimination still persists.

African American families comprise a variety of structures, with a large number of female-headed households. Some scholars (Billingsley, 1994; Hill, 1972, 1977, 1993, 1994, 1999a, 1999b; Logan, 2001; Staples & Johnson, 1993) did extensive research on the Black family to demonstrate its strength and to lessen the pathological framework used by many authors (Moynihan, 1965; Jensen, 1985; Herrnstein & Murray, 1994). Herrnstein and Murray stated that the persistent achievement gap between rich and poor children and Black and white children was deeply rooted in intelligence; hence, intelligence was inherited and probably genetic and that society should accept this fact. This statement was experienced as a major assault by the African American community. Dr. Robert Hill, a well-known social worker, identified five family strengths which constitute for Blacks "adaptations" that are necessary for survival in a hostile environment. These strengths may also be found in other families, but are particularly relevant for Black families. The strengths are as follows: (1) strong kinship bonds; (2) strong work orientation; (3) adaptability of family roles, which is a response to economic survival; (4) high achievement orientation; and (5) a strong religious belief system. These strengths are important to understand in making an assessment of Black families and can be used to support their vulnerabilities (Hill, 1972).

Historically, strong kinship bonds in Black families were seen when Black families took in relatives' children as well as children of close friends who were considered family. The extended Black family included both kin and non-kin and served as a support system for all parties involved. Hill's focus on strong work orientation was important because it dispelled the misrepresentation by social scientists that African Americans were lazy and did not work, preferring to be on welfare. Hill maintained that the welfare system was often used by African Americans because of job discrimination and the unavailability of jobs. Hill saw the thesis of African Americans not wanting to work as being an unfair representation; in fact, he noted that it was quite common for Black women to be employed long before this became a norm for white women.

Flexibility in African American families was borne out of economic necessity based on the need for both members of a parental couple to work. Sometimes fathers worked nights so that mothers could work during the day, in order to secure a decent income for the family (Hill, 1972). High achievement and valuing of education has often been negatively reported on by mainstream researchers. The devaluing of high achievement by Blacks does not take into account the ways in which Black families pushed their children to achieve at the level that their resources allowed. As well, they taught their children to have confidence and a strong sense of self, despite the negative messages given by the majority culture. For Black families, education was seen as "the ticket" out of poverty. Religion and spirituality is very highly valued by the Black family and is a major survival skill. African American families turn to religion and spirituality as a way of coping with the reality of the hostile environment. The church was a place where one could talk about one's pains, sorrows, and heartbreaks, and through catharsis release many pent-up feelings (Hill, 1972, 1999a).

Hispanics or Latinos

Although the word "Hispanic" is often used to refer to Spanish-speaking immigrants and their descendants, the term "Latino" is now preferred because it references their prior Hispanic identity. Latinos tend to place high regard on community, modesty, cooperation, and hierarchical relationships. They value the family (*familismo*) and see the family as being of greater importance than the individual. In large numbers of Latino families, grandparents, uncles, aunts, and cousins live with or near the nuclear family. Even when Latinos leave their country of origin and come to the United States to work, they typically send a percentage of their earnings home to support the family members there. Family members are protective of and loyal to each other. In Latino families, it is often expected that children will take care of parents when they are sick or aging. Latinos value interpersonal relationships and are likely to want to develop a more personal type of relationship with you as a social worker. Latinos tend to prefer being kind and courteous and tend to avoid conflict. Gender roles are clearly defined, with the wife being the homemaker/caregiver and the husband being the provider and protector of the family. The word *machismo* is used by Latino families to designate the male role as primary and as demonstrating maleness and virility (Sue, 2006). The female counterpart, *marianismo*, means morally spiritual and able to endure great suffering (Garcia-Preto, 1996). Catholicism is the major religion for Hispanics.

Native Americans

Native Americans were the first U.S. settlers, although their land was gradually taken from them by way of treaties and agreements, which were later broken, by the early colonists. When land was taken from the Native Americans by the government, their way of life changed considerably, and left a negative impact on the Native American population. In 1959 the Children's Bureau and the Child Welfare League of America supported legislation known as the Indian Adoption Project (Palmiste, 2008). This project started the push for white families to adopt Native American children who were being raised either in foster care or in federal boarding homes. Schools for Native Americans were developed which resulted in their being forced to leave their families and attend boarding schools, which required that they live either at the boarding schools or with white families. The Indian Removal Act of 1830 was the first act that allowed the removal of Native American children from their homes. This act had the greatest impact on tribes located in the South, where more states were enforcing the law to acquire land. This was a major disruption to Native American family life and was to represent a major assault to the psychological development of Native American children.

In addition to the emotional trauma experienced by the children, many of them had serious health problems that ended in death. It is estimated that one out of every eleven Native American children died while residing at a boarding school, and one out of every five children died shortly upon their return from schools (DeJong, 2007). The schools were often not equipped with proper medical supplies and children were often forced to work in return for their board. The children were taught from a European American perspective, and in addition were expected to clean the living quarters, make their own clothing and shoes, and farm and harvest their own food. These requirements were carried out to "Americanize" the Native American children.

The Indian Child Welfare Act of 1978 was passed and charged welfare workers with the task of notifying Native American parents and their tribes or reservations of the removal of a Native American child (Palmiste, 2008). This act allowed the tribal councils to have control over a child's placement, and the act gave the local governments the responsibility of ensuring that each child had an attorney to represent his or her best interest. All of the above circumstances resulted in the current cycle of poverty seen among Native Americans and the high alcoholism rate. Disruption in parenting practices also impacted Native American family life.

Asian Americans and Pacific Islanders

Asian Americans and Pacific Islander families are in the process of acculturating to American society. They are seen as being competent and placing a high value on education and learning. They exercise restraint and deference to their parents and the elderly. They tend to maintain remnants of their cultural beliefs, rituals, and special celebrations and see these as a source of identity and strength. Family is important to Asian Americans/Pacific Islanders and the family is typical patriarchal, with the father serving as head of the family and the mother as caregiver. Sons are typically valued more than daughters, and the child is expected to obey the family and to respect the elderly. They emphasize the importance of one's immediate and extended family.

Children are expected to succeed and to bring honor to the family. If a family member is in trouble it brings shame not just to the individual family member but to the family as a whole. Modesty is valued, and sensitivity to the family name is highly valued. It is important to note whether a family is first, second, third, or fourth generation in the United States, as this helps to clarify the extent of their acculturation. The more acculturated they are, the more integrated in American culture they will tend to be. This will be helpful to you when you are making an assessment and developing an intervention strategy.

The four minority groups listed above, and other oppressed groups to include women, poor and working-class families, gays and lesbians, persons with mental illnesses, persons with disabilities, persons who are aging, and illegal immigrants, all typically suffer from marginalization and discrimination. Marginalized groups refer to those groups that are relatively powerless due to socioeconomics, class, age cohort, race and ethnicity, or religion. These groups are seen as having lesser importance than the dominant group. These groups are also typically discriminated against, meaning that they experience negative treatment based on their race, gender, religion, or ethnicity.

A large percentage of persons who are oppressed also suffer from poverty. There were 36 million African American people in the United States as of March 2002. This constituted 13% of the population. Yet, African Americans accounted for about 8.1 million of the population in poverty in 2001. There were 12.5 million Asian Americans living in the United States in March 2002, which represented 4.4% of the population, and approximately 10%, or 1.3 million, Asian Americans lived in poverty. In 2002, there were 37.4 million Latinos in the United States, representing 13.3% of the population. In this same year, 21.4% of Latinos lived in poverty. Native Americans made up 2.3 million people in the United States in 2002. Seventy-five percent (75%) of the Native American workforce earned less than $7,000 annually, with 45% of Native Americans living below the poverty level. These statistics are appalling given the richness of this country. Many of your clients will represent families who live in poverty, and you will need to empower them and advocate on their behalf. You will also learn to identify and define forms of oppression and to examine structural forces that systematically interfere with the progress of these oppressed groups toward achieving social and economic justice.

Your ability to empower ethnic minority families and other client populations will be important in your role as a social worker. Barker (2003, p. 142) defines empowerment as "the process of helping individuals, families, groups, and communities increase their personal, interpersonal, socioeconomic, and political strength and develop influence toward improving their circumstances." Empowerment has personal, interpersonal, and structural dimensions that apply to social systems at all levels (Rappaport, 1987). Personal empowerment means your own sense of competence, mastery, strength, and ability to affect change. Interpersonal empowerment refers to your ability to influence others through interactions with them. Structural empowerment will involve your relationships with social and political structures in order to bring about change for your clients. When people interact with those in their environment, it increases their access to control and resources. You will serve as an advocate for your client and will empower them to seek resources on their behalf.

In learning to work with families who are diverse and impoverished, you will have to become culturally competent as mandated by the NASW Indicators for the Achievement of the NASW Standards for Cultural Competence (2008). To become culturally competent, you will need to develop knowledge and skills in the following areas: (1) knowledge of ethnic and racial identity development; (2) knowledge of values, beliefs, and cultural practices of ethnic groups; (3) ability to respect and appreciate the values and beliefs of all clients, including culturally different clients; (4) knowledge of the processes of immigration and acculturation; (5) knowledge of poverty, marginalization, alienation, privilege, and power; and (6) ability to change your beliefs, assumptions, and stereotypes. You will also need to understand and appreciate discrimination as it relates to age, class, color, culture, disability, ethnicity, gender identity and expression, sexual orientation, race, religion, and political ideology (Pinderhughes, 1997, 2000).

You will also need to be aware of your own cultural values and bias, and have knowledge and understanding of how oppression, sexism, and homophobia affect you personally and acknowledge your own beliefs and feelings about these matters. You must be knowledgeable about your own racial, class, cultural, and sexual orientation. You must also be willing to seek out educational, consultative, and training experiences that enrich your cross-cultural experiences to enhance your cultural competence. This will require you to be self-reflective, to respect indigenous helping practices, and to be knowledgeable about potential biases in assessment and testing instruments. This means that you must be familiar with research and latest findings regarding mental health issues of diverse groups.

UNDERSTANDING OF KNOWLEDGE

Please choose the *best* answer from among the possible choices.

1. The United States is undergoing a major demographic shift referred to as:

    a. A pluralistic society
    b. The "browning" and "graying" of America
    c. A male-dominated society
    d. A female-dominated society

2. Diversity content in MSW programs should:

    a. Be integrated throughout the curriculum
    b. Be an "add-on" course
    c. Be only in human behavior and the environment
    d. Be only in social policy

3. Social workers are governed by:

   a. The NASW Code of Ethics
   b. Counseling standards
   c. NASW Code of Ethics and NASW Standards for Cultural Competence in Social Work
   d. Council on Social Work Education Indicators

4. The NASW Standards for Cultural Competence include all of the following *except*:

   a. Self-awareness and cross-cultural knowledge
   b. Cross-cultural skills
   c. Language diversity
   d. Reflective listening

5. Oppression is defined as:

   a. Valuing privilege
   b. Temporary or permanent reduction in functioning
   c. The social act of placing severe restrictions on an individual, group, or institution
   d. A condition in which the system is not functioning properly

6. The current fastest-growing ethnic minority group in the United States is:

   a. Latinos
   b. African Americans
   c. Native Americans
   d. Asian Americans

7. Dr. Robert Hill identified five strengths of African American families, which include all *except*:

   a. Strong kinship bonds and work orientation
   b. Strong focus on community
   c. Adaptability of family roles
   d. Strong religious belief system

8. The Indian Child Welfare Act of 1978 was passed and charged welfare workers with:

   a. The task of allowing child welfare workers to remove children without parental consent.
   b. The task of allowing children to request removal from their home due to parental abuse.
   c. The task of allowing relatives to determine that children could be removed from their homes.
   d. The task of notifying Native American parents and their tribes or reservations of the removal of a Native American child.

9. The ethnic group that is seen as being competent and placing a high value on education and learning, as well as exercising restraint and deference to their parents and the elderly, is:

   a. African Americans
   b. Hispanics/Latinos
   c. Asian Americans
   d. Native Americans

10. *Marginalized groups* refer to those groups that are:

    a. Relatively powerless due to socioeconomics, class, age cohort, race and ethnicity, or religion.
    b. Enormously privileged, powerful, and capable of creating large numbers of political and social changes.
    c. Largely religious, with moderate ability to influence parishioners and community residents.
    d. People who are able to have significant impact on legislation and state and national policies.

11. To be culturally competent you would need all of the following *except*:

    a. Knowledge of ethnic and racial identity development
    b. Knowledge of the processes of immigration and acculturation
    c. Knowledge of poverty, marginalization, alienation, privilege, and power
    d. Knowledge of preexisting developmental issues

12. A large percentage of persons who are oppressed also suffer from:

    a. Poverty
    b. Discrimination
    c. Marginalization
    d. All of the above

13. The word *machismo* is used by Latino families to designate the male role as:

    a. Demonstrating weakness and fearfulness
    b. Demonstrating strong feelings of morality
    c. Primary and as demonstrating maleness and virility
    d. Demonstrating a love for children

14. The past and current treatment of Native Americans has led to:

    a. More educational and cultural advantages
    b. Dysfunctional families and high levels of alcoholism
    c. Greater respect and sense of fairness
    d. An increase in political representation

15. Empowerment includes all of the following dimensions *except*:

    a. Personal
    b. Interpersonal
    c. Structural
    d. Political

MASTERY AND ASSESSMENT OF KNOWLEDGE OF SKILLS

Please choose the *best* answer from among the possible choices.

1. A six-year-old Latina female child recently moved from Mexico with her mother and grandmother. No one in the family speaks English. When the grandmother talks with the child, the child responds in English. The grandmother punishes the child for using English rather than Spanish. The school social worker should first:

    a. Remove the child from the home to an English-speaking foster home.
    b. Explore the family customs and why they want the child to speak Spanish in the home.
    c. Speak with the family and insist that the child speak English at home.
    d. Suggest to the family that they learn English.

2. A Native American client seeks help at a family agency because his wife threatens to divorce him if he does not seek counseling. The client admits that he has a drinking problem that causes him to strike out in anger at his wife. What does the social worker deal with first?

    a. The husband's drinking problem
    b. The husband's anger
    c. The husband's feelings about his wife's threats to divorce
    d. The wife's desire to divorce him

3. A seven-year-old African American client wants the school social worker to agree to keep a secret about her fighting in school from her mother. The school social worker should assure the child that she:

   a. Will keep confidentiality and will not tell the mother without discussing it with her first.
   b. Will tell the mother because she wants the mother to help the child with her anger.
   c. Will keep the information secret as well as other information the child discloses.
   d. Will tell the mother and the child's teachers.

4. A fifteen-year-old Asian adolescent is in conflict with her family because her behavior is "too American" (she wants to date, attend parties, smoke, and drink). The social worker should:

   a. Discuss with the client the differences in values between the cultures and generations and that her parents are attempting to reconcile these differences and to aid her in age-appropriate activities.
   b. Tell the client that she is fifteen and should be allowed to do what her peers are doing.
   c. Encourage the client to have the neighbors talk to her parents.
   d. Encourage the client to wait until she is 18 and able to make her own decisions.

5. An African American wife is having an affair with a man who is not her husband. She has told the social worker she will not tell her husband and will continue the affair. The social worker should:

   a. Break the confidentiality and inform the husband.
   b. Terminate the treatment with the wife.
   c. Continue to see the wife and encourage her to tell her husband.
   d. Tell the wife to have a friend tell the husband.

6. A Latina female client informs her social worker that she is also seeing a folk healer. The social worker should:

   a. Tell the client that she has to make a choice between the folk healer and the social worker.
   b. Tell the client that she has to terminate treatment.
   c. Tell the client that she will continue treatment and that the folk healing can complement the treatment.
   d. Tell the client that she must stop seeing the folk healer.

7. An African American historical neighborhood is being torn down. The families being displaced will more likely adjust to their new homes if:

   a. They have input in the selection of the homes.
   b. The homes are selected by city council.
   c. The homes will allow all neighbors to remain together.
   d. The homes are located near a church.

8. A Latino family has requested couples counseling at a family service agency. The couple brings the wife's parents to the initial session. The social worker should:

   a. Tell the wife's parents that they cannot participate in the session.
   b. Allow the parents to attend the session given the important role they play, and based on that session, determine who will attend future sessions.
   c. Tell the parents that their presence is intrusive.
   d. Cancel the session because the parents are present.

9. A couple you are counseling on relationship issues tells you how appreciative they are to you—that they would not have made it had it not been for you, and that you are an extraordinary therapist. You should:

   a. Thank the couple for their wonderful compliments.
   b. Tell the couple that they did the difficult part of treatment and the credit belongs with them.
   c. Tell the couple that should they have future problems, you would welcome seeing them again.
   d. Minimize the therapeutic treatment process.

10. An African American member of the social work staff of a large agency that serves a very diverse population has been asked to offer training on cultural sensitivity for all social work staff. The social worker should:

    a. Seek out an expert in the field to work with her.
    b. Contact all members of the staff for a brainstorming session.
    c. Develop a workshop that focuses on African American clients only.
    d. Design a comprehensive training program focused on cultural sensitivity that will have as a main goal the development of cultural competence by all participants.

11. A female client is in her first session with you. She identifies herself as lesbian and indicates that she wants to see a social worker who is also lesbian. You should:

   a. Ask her why she would like to see a social worker who is lesbian.
   b. Refer her to a social worker who is lesbian.
   c. Reassure the client that you have worked with lesbians in the past and can continue to see her.
   d. Explain that from your experience, one does not have to be lesbian to be helpful to a lesbian client.

12. An African American social worker, who appears to be pregnant, is seeking employment at a large mental health agency. She is interviewed by the director, who asks her a series of questions. Which question is appropriate to ask?

   a. Are you from a single-parent home?
   b. Are you married?
   c. What is your social security number?
   d. Do you have other children?

A social work professor of an MSW program was discussing a case study of a Latino family of Mexican American background. The daughter in the family, Maria, age 25, is a college graduate, employed as a teacher in an elementary school, and living at home with her parents and 19-year-old brother, José, who is in college. As part of the case discussion, the professor indicated that Maria is experiencing separation issues because she is overly dependent on her parents, which demonstrates an enmeshed family. The professor stated that most employed 25 year olds have their own apartments and are living on their own. A Latino student questioned the professor about his statement, indicating that Maria's situation is not unusual in Latino families. She was supported by the other minority students and some of the majority students, who stated that a 25-year-old female staying at home might also be seen as appropriate in other cultures. The African American students indicated that this circumstance was prevalent for Black families as well.

The professor stated that healthy development necessitated that family members who reach the age of maturity typically separate from their families, which avoids boundary issues among family members. The professor further stated that enmeshed families do not allow for family members to be independent. The Latino student and other members of the class continued to protest the professor's comment, stating that families can be close and supportive of each other without being enmeshed. The professor's frustration and anger began to show, and he lectured the class that development is universal; that just because an ethnic group practices certain behaviors does not mean that it is psychologically healthy.

13. The professor's statement is problematic because:

    a. There is no evidence of psychological enmeshment and many young adults remain at home following college for a number of reasons.
    b. The professor's comments are correct in that development is the same across cultures.
    c. The students do not have the right to question a professor.
    d. The Latino students do not understand their own cultural background.

14. The professor's statements do not reflect the values of Latino families or the NASW Standards of Cultural Competence because:

    a. His responses do not take student opinions into account.
    b. His responses violate Standard 3 – Cross-Cultural Knowledge.
    c. His statements do not reflect what other professors teach.
    d. His statements do not reflect what he taught last semester.

15. As a social worker, you must be able to share the worldview of the culturally diverse clients in your agency. An elderly Asian client, Ms. Chin, has recently come to this country to live with her daughter. She fell and broke her hip while climbing the stairs in her daughter's home. Ms. Chin requires surgery, which will mean that she has to remain in the hospital for several weeks for rehabilitation. Ms. Chin wants to return to her daughter's home following surgery, but the doctor feels that the family cannot manage Ms. Chin's rehabilitation in their home. The medical social worker can best address this situation by:

    a. Explaining the hospital procedures and requirements.
    b. Insisting that the hospital recommendations cannot be changed.
    c. Explaining that the hospital cannot do the surgery if Ms. Chin cannot remain for the rehabilitation.
    d. Talking with Ms. Chin and her daughter about potential alternatives that will take into account the Asian cultural values and attitudes regarding elderly care postsurgery.

Reflective Essay Questions

1. Compare and contrast ways in which you feel your field placement promotes and practices diversity in its physical environment (accessibility to persons with disabilities), written materials (reading materials, artwork, etc., that appeal to diverse groups of people), as well as staffing patterns (extent to which it is reflective of population served in terms of percentage or ratio).

2. Discuss some of your biases, prejudices, and/or ignorance regarding diverse groups and detail the steps you utilize in attempts to identify and overcome them. Discuss how this affects your learning experience in the class and practice experience in the field at your internship.

3. Discuss the pros and cons in which you feel your MSW program promotes and practices diversity in its physical environment (unwritten policies and practices, artwork, language adaptations, etc.), policies and procedures (field agency selections, graduate assistantship selections, etc.), as well as staffing patterns (visual representation of people from a variety of backgrounds, etc.).

4. Discuss and identify which racial or ethnic population or populations you currently prefer not work with and why?

5. Discuss your earliest recollections of the negative and positive characteristics attributed to your gender, race, ethnicity, socioeconomic status, and spirituality. Identify whom the memories are attributable to, how you were affected by them, and what impact they have had on your current understanding and sensitivity to diversity.

5

HUMAN RIGHTS & JUSTICE

DETAILED UNDERSTANDING AND EXPLANATION (DUE)

Human rights and justice are recognizable concepts that you studied in your liberal arts courses as an undergraduate, and are terms that you will study in detail while in your MSW programs. Civil and constitutional rights, or privileges and civil liberties, are but a few words to describe human rights. Therefore, human rights are the privileges, opportunities, and freedoms that should be afforded to all humans regardless of race, ethnicity, socioeconomic status, culture, national origin, religion, physical ability, sexual orientation, age, class, veteran status, political ideology, mental status, and/or lifestyle. As first-year social work students, you will discuss at length in your policy and human behavior classes the civil liberties, legal rights, and constitutionality of some actions to which disenfranchised groups and/or populations at risk fall victim. Fairness and impartiality, or honesty and integrity, are familiar terms that convey justice; however, justice revolves around a simple question: "Is this fair?" Bell (1997) offers a vision of a just society as a "society in which the distribution of resources is equitable and all members are physically and psychologically safe and secure." Consequently, justice is a set of universal principles that guide people in judging what is right and what is wrong, no matter what culture and society they live in. In other words, it is the worldwide philosophy which influences people's decisions regarding that which is right and that which is wrong, regardless of customs, traditions, or *their social order* (CESJ, 2010).

In 1948, the General Assembly of the United Nations adopted the Universal Declaration of Human Rights (UDHR) as the first universal statement on the basic principles of absolute human rights, and stated in clear and simple terms the rights that belong equally to every person. They identified thirty articles of common standards of achievement for all people, of which eleven are presented below as being central principles to your understanding regarding human rights during your first year as an MSW student. They are engrained in the fabric of the NASW Code of Ethics, which is the command for social workers to challenge social injustice and pursue "social change," mainly for vulnerable and oppressed individuals and groups of people. As an explanation of one of the essential systems of belief of the social work profession, the eleven articles of the Universal Declaration of Human Rights (1948) are as follows:

Article 2 – Freedom

Everyone is entitled to all the rights and freedoms set forth in this Declaration, without distinction of any kind, such as race, color, sex, language, religion, political or other opinion, national or social origin, property, birth, or other status. Furthermore, no distinction shall be made on the basis of the political, jurisdictional, or international status of the country or territory to which a person belongs, whether it is independent, trust, non-self-governing, or under any other limitation of sovereignty.

Article 3 – Safety

Everyone has the right to life, liberty, and security of person.

Article 7 – Protection of the Law

All are equal before the law and are entitled without any discrimination to equal protection of the law. All are entitled to equal protection against any discrimination in violation of this Declaration and against any incitement to such discrimination.

Article 12 – Privacy

No one shall be subjected to arbitrary interference with his privacy, family, home, or correspondence, or to attacks upon his honor and reputation. Everyone has the right to the protection of the law against such interference or attacks.

Article 17 – Access to Housing

(1) Everyone has the right to own property alone as well as in association with others.

(2) No one shall be arbitrarily deprived of his property.

Article 18 – Freedom of Religion

Everyone has the right to freedom of thought, conscience, and religion; this right includes freedom to change his religion or belief, and freedom, either alone or in community with others and in public or private, to manifest his religion or belief in teaching, practice, worship, and observance.

Article 21 – Access to Public Services

(2) Everyone has the right of equal access to public service in his country.

(3) The will of the people shall be the basis of the authority of government; this will shall be expressed in periodic and genuine elections which shall be by universal and equal suffrage and shall be held by secret vote or by equivalent free voting procedures.

Article 22 – Access to Economic, Social, and Cultural Rights

Everyone, as a member of society, has the right to social security and is entitled to realization, through national effort and international cooperation and in accordance with the organization and resources of each State, of the economic, social, and cultural rights indispensable for his dignity and the free development of his personality.

Article 23 – Access to Adequate Standard of Living

(1) Everyone has the right to work, to free choice of employment, to just and favorable conditions of work, and to protection against unemployment.

(2) Everyone, without any discrimination, has the right to equal pay for equal work.
(3) Everyone who works has the right to just and favorable remuneration ensuring for himself and his family an existence worthy of human dignity, and supplemented, if necessary, by other means of social protection.
(4) Everyone has the right to form and to join trade unions for the protection of his interests.

Article 25 – Access to Adequate Standard of Living Including Healthcare

(1) Everyone has the right to a standard of living adequate for the health and well-being of himself and of his family, including food, clothing, housing, and medical care and necessary social services, and the right to security in the event of unemployment, sickness, disability, widowhood, old age, or other lack of livelihood in circumstances beyond his control.

(2) Motherhood and childhood are entitled to special care and assistance. All children, whether born in or out of wedlock, shall enjoy the same social protection.

Article 26 – Access to Education

(1) Everyone has the right to education. Education shall be free, at least in the elementary and fundamental stages. Elementary education shall be compulsory. Technical and professional education shall be made generally available and higher education shall be equally accessible to all on the basis of merit.

(2) Education shall be directed to the full development of the human personality and to the strengthening of respect for human rights and fundamental freedoms. It shall promote understanding, tolerance, and friendship among all nations, racial or religious groups, and shall further the activities of the United Nations for the maintenance of peace.

(3) Parents have a prior right to choose the kind of education that shall be given to their children.

In 2008, the National Association of Social Work (NASW) observed the 60th anniversary of the United Nations Universal Declaration of Human Rights with a renewed dedication to support and advocate for human rights concerns (NASW, 2008). Commitment to human rights has been the core of the social work profession and will be a major foundation in which you will support and advocate for your clients. You will learn in your MSW introductory courses conceptual frameworks that address the foundational knowledge, values, and skills associated with social work and the ethical standards and principles according to the Code of Ethics. As social work students, you will learn methods to utilize as well as techniques to adopt in your endeavors to competently advocate for the human rights, social justice, and economic fairness of your clients and will integrate them in your field placements during your practicum experiences.

You will also learn that while the concept of social justice, at a glance, seems readily apparent, there are many meanings (CESJ, 2010; Chambers &

Wedel, 2009; Netting, Kettner, & McMurtry, 2008) but no agreed-on definition of social justice. You will discuss and research the theories and models of social justice in class with your professors and via research assignments. You will also explore the principles of social justice and investigate its values with your clients during your practicum experience as issues arise with individuals, families, and groups you work with in your agency field placements. During your foundation year, you will learn about your responsibilities to promote social justice within society and on behalf of your clients. You will learn how to advocate for your client when faced with the realities of discrimination, the challenges of cultural incompetence, and the proliferation of unequal rights within the agencies at which you intern and will possibly one day be employed. Regarding social justice, DuBois and Miley (2011) affirm that it "prevails when all members of a society share equally in the social order, secure an equitable consideration of resources and opportunities, and enjoy their full benefit of civil liberties" (p. 16). Oppression is "the systematic, institutionalized mistreatment of one group of people by another for whatever reason" (Yamato, 1993, p. 207). This causes these oppressed individuals or groups with minority status to be devalued, exploited, and deprived of privileges by the individuals or majority groups who have more power. Oppression then results in a disparity of power between the identified majority population and groups with minority status, which in so doing denies them access to opportunities and resources, thereby limiting their rightful participation in society (DuBois & Miley, 2011). You will also learn in your foundation coursework that the concept of oppression involves putting extreme limitations and constraints on some persons, groups, or large systems and that primary and secondary oppression are several widely accepted models of oppression (Brittan & Maynard, 1984; Rogers, 2006). Primary oppression refers to the "direct consequences of perceived group differences"; whereas, secondary oppression refers to "a deeper awareness of oppression by those who are oppressed that goes beyond the obvious consequences." Any policy that considers that women are biologically inferior to men and therefore should not be afforded the same rights would be an example of primary oppression; while an African American who is denied housing who recognizes the oppression structure that supports that action, but does not need this action put into logical or analytical terms, is an example of secondary oppression (Rogers, 2006, p. 118).

Discrimination has taken on many forms in American history, and it is important that in your foundation year you not only grasp an understanding of it but of concepts and theories relative to prejudice, racism, and economic deprivation. In order to better serve your clients in your field placements, you must be able to critically think in your coursework as well as utilize the application of these theories when considering factors that might affect your clients in your field practicum. Discrimination is negatively treating an individual, family, or group differently based on preconceived notions about them. In the case of your client base, it is basically treating people who have been identified as the "populations at risk" differently based on the fact that they belong to some group rather than on their merit. Populations at risk can be defined as groups of people who share some identifiable characteristic that places them at greater risk of social and economic deprivation and oppression than the general mainstream of society. These include people "distinguished by age, ethnicity, culture, class, religion, and physical or mental disability" and such groups as "people of color, women, and gay and lesbian persons" (Kirst-Ashman, 2007; CSWE, 2008).

It is important for you to be able to distinguish between discrimination, prejudice, and racism early within your foundation year. Prejudice can be thought of as negative attitudes based on false beliefs that can become the basis for discriminatory actions. It means to prejudge, to make a judgment in advance of due examination. For example, the generalization that noncustodial African American fathers in your community are not active in their children's lives, which results in excluding them from opportunities to participate in fatherhood initiative programs, is an example of a prejudicial belief resulting in a discriminatory action. In the case of the noncustodial father, you based your decision on that in which you believed and did not prove and consequentially did not work toward an end that would include him. There is no single explanation for prejudice; rather there exist several theoretical conceptualizations for its origin, which you will learn in detail in your advanced year in your MSW program. You will learn how to approach prejudice from several different perspectives that will provide insight into your clients' problems and situations.

Racism and economic deprivation are additional phenomenon that you will encounter in your foundation field placement as you work with your clients. Racism involves labeling of people based on their race. DuBois & Miley (2011) describe racism as the "ideology that perpetuates the social domination of one racial group by another" (p. 139). In your first-year MSW courses you will further learn about different forms of racism such as aversive, individual, and institutional racism and their affect on your clients' attitude toward your service delivery to them while at your field placement. Hudson, Dovidio, and Gaertner (2004) define the concept of *aversive racism* as a subtle form of bias existing below conscious deliberation, which allows an individual to discriminate as long as the situation allows him or her to "maintain a positive view of the self," which often manifests itself as a preference for one's own group and avoidance of other groups, often to their detriment. Aversive racism is difficult to combat, since those practicing it are unlikely to acknowledge personal prejudices (Jimenez, 2010; Hudson, Dovidio, & Gaertner, 2004). Individual racism is the negative ideas, thoughts, and actions of a person, either unconscious or conscious, that support or facilitate racism both actively and passively. During your foundation year you will guard against falling victim to individual racism by participating in open and honest dialogue with your professors and cohort, as well as processing self-reflective exercises during weekly supervision with your school advisor and/or agency supervisor.

Institutional racism, in contrast, involves the blatant or covert labeling and mistreatment of people based on their race through unfair policies, unjust procedures, and unmerited practices by public or private agencies, organizations, or institutions. Institutional racism results in public laws and regulations that are used to differentiate and discriminate according to race. You will learn, firsthand, about the magnitude of poverty among the families that you will serve in your field placements and the economic deprivation and institutional inequalities that exist among them. Economic deprivation or the lack of sufficient income to meet basic needs contributes to the persistent problem of poverty. This directly opposes the concept of economic justice, which is the principle stating that everyone should be afforded the same opportunities and access to the fair allocations of resources essential to live to their human best. Social and economic forces produce different family relationships. Clients whom you will work with who are part of different socioeconomic structures have different connections with institutions and different ways of acquiring the necessities of life. "The ultimate purpose of economic justice is to free each person to engage creatively in the unlimited work beyond economics" (CESJ, 2010). The lack of financially viability and economic autonomy of your clients oftentimes results in frustration and irritation that can lead to the lack of social support for working parents and their children, child abuse, spousal abuse, or illegal activity to generate cash and other social ills that you will discuss in your classes and interact with in your field placements.

You will learn that discrimination, prejudice, racism, and economic deprivation subsist within the complex network of cultural, economic, and institutional structures in the communities that you will be working with for many of your clients. No single theory provides a complete picture as to why discrimination, prejudice, racism, or economic deprivation occur, but the sources of these injustices are both internal and external to those who are victims of them. As a social work student, you will begin to recognize the global interconnection of oppression, discrimination, and institutional inequalities and how your client's membership in a population at risk largely affects their life experiences and worldview as well as increases risk factors for exposure to discrimination and economic stress. In your first-year MSW courses you will learn the importance of securing firm foundational knowledge of ethical standards in addition to gaining an understanding of human rights as espoused by the profession. You will also learn the importance of essential culturally sensitive practice for service delivery and intervention development for your clients.

UNDERSTANDING OF KNOWLEDGE

Please choose the *best* answer from among the possible choices.

1. In 1948, the first universal statement on the basic principles of absolute human rights, that stated in clear and simple terms the rights that belong equally to every person; acknowledged that inherent dignity, equal privileges, and inalienable rights were "the foundation of freedom, justice and peace in the world"; and that these civil rights should be protected by the rule of the law, was the:

    a. National Association of Social Workers – NASW
    b. Council on Social Work Education – CSWE
    c. General Assembly of the United Nations Universal Declaration of Human Rights – UDHR
    d. The United States Declaration of Independence

2. All of the following are terms that describe human rights, *except*:

    a. Constitutional rights
    b. Privileges
    c. Narrow-mindedness
    d. Civil rights

3. Article 22 of the Universal Declaration of Human Rights, which addresses "Access to Economic, Social and Cultural Rights" and is supported by the NASW, is *best* identified as:

    a. Everyone has the right to form and to join trade unions for the protection of his interests.
    b. Everyone has the right to freedom of thought, conscience, and religion; this right includes freedom to change his religion or belief, and freedom, either alone or in community with others and in public or private, to manifest his religion or belief in teaching, practice, worship, and observance.
    c. Everyone, as a member of society, has the right to social security and is entitled to realization, through national effort and international cooperation and in accordance with the organization and resources of each State, of the economic, social, and cultural rights indispensable for his dignity and the free development of his personality.
    d. Everyone has the right to life, liberty, and security of person.

4. The principle of fairness and equity, especially in accordance with moral and ethical rightness, social standard, and law, as well as guiding people in judging what is right and what is wrong, no matter what culture and society they live in, is best known as:

   a. Discrimination
   b. Prejudice
   c. Justice
   d. Human rights

5. All of the following are articles of the common standards of achievement by the United Nations Universal Declaration of Human Rights that address Article 26 – Access to Education, *except*:

   a. Everyone has the right to education. Education shall be free, at least in the elementary and fundamental stages. Elementary education shall be compulsory. Technical and professional education shall be made generally available and higher education shall be equally accessible to all on the basis of merit.
   b. Parents have a prior right to choose the kind of education that shall be given to their children.
   c. No one shall be subjected to arbitrary interference with his privacy, family, home, or correspondence, or to attacks upon his honor and reputation. Everyone has the right to the protection of the law against such interference or attacks.
   d. Education shall be directed to the full development of the human personality and to the strengthening of respect for human rights and fundamental freedoms. It shall promote understanding, tolerance, and friendship among all nations, racial or religious groups, and shall further the activities of the United Nations for the maintenance of peace.

6. The opportunity to be accorded the same prerogatives and obligations in social fulfillment as are accorded to all others without distinction as to race, gender, language, or religion is best defined as:

   a. Economic justice   c. Oppression
   b. Human right   d. Institutional inequity

7. The subtle form of bias existing below conscious deliberation, which allows an individual to discriminate as long as the situation allows him or her to "maintain a positive view of the self," and often manifests itself as a preferences for one's own group and avoidance of other groups, often to their detriment, is best known as:

   a. Prejudice
   b. Institutional racism
   c. Aversive racism
   d. Economic justice

8. Discrimination is a concept that is opposed by many professions, particularly social work; however, as it relates to your clients, it is treating "populations at risk" based on their group affiliation and not on their merit. In this regard, discrimination is *best* defined as:

   a. Labeling of people based on their race.
   b. The prejudgment and negative treatment of people based on identifiable characteristics such as race, gender, religion, or ethnicity.
   c. Stereotyping and generalizing about people because of their race.
   d. A bias against members of a racial group and belief that these group's genetic (racial) physical characteristics are linked in a direct causal way to psychological, intellectual, or behavioral traits that distinguish superior and inferior groups.

9. All of the following are terms that convey justice, *except*:

   a. Stereotyping and generalizing
   b. Fairness and impartiality
   c. Honesty and integrity
   d. Equality and sameness

10. The term used for groups of people who share some identifiable characteristic that places them at greater risk of social and economic deprivation and oppression than the general mainstream of society is best known as:

    a. People of color and women
    b. Gay and lesbian persons
    c. Populations at risk
    d. Group stereotyping and generalizing

11. Article 25 of the Universal Declaration of Human Rights, which addresses "Adequate Standard of Living Including Healthcare" is *best* identified as:

    a. Everyone who works has the right to just and favorable remuneration ensuring for himself and his family an existence worthy of human dignity, and supplemented, if necessary, by other means of social protection.
    b. Everyone has the right to a standard of living adequate for the health and well-being of himself and of his family, including food, clothing, housing, and medical care and necessary social services, and the right to security in the event of unemployment, sickness, disability, widowhood, old age, or other lack of livelihood in circumstances beyond his control.
    c. Everyone has the right of equal access to public service in his country.
    d. Everyone has the right to work, to free choice of employment, to just and favorable conditions of work, and to protection against unemployment.

12. The ideal condition in which all members of society have the same basic rights, protections, opportunities, obligations, and social benefits is best known as:

   a. Social justice
   b. Justice
   c. Discrimination
   d. Economic deprivation

13. Prejudice can be thought of as:

   a. Negative attitudes one person has about all members of a racial or ethnic group that often result in overt acts such as name calling, social exclusion, or violence.
   b. Negative attitudes based on false beliefs that can become the basis for discriminatory actions which cause one to prejudge, to make a judgment in advance of due examination.
   c. Policies, practices, or procedures embedded in bureaucratic structures that systematically lead to unequal outcomes for people of color.
   d. The disparity of power between the identified majority population and groups with minority status, which denies them access to opportunities and resources thereby limiting their rightful participation in society.

14. As a key social work value, social justice will involve all of the following *except*:

   a. Advocating and confronting oppression.
   b. Being an opponent of discrimination.
   c. Participating in institutional inequities.
   d. Defending against aversive racism.

15. The article of common standards of achievement by the UDHR that states that all are equal before the law and are entitled without any discrimination to equal protection of the law and equal protection against any discrimination is best known as:

   a. Article 12 – Privacy
   b. Article 7 – Protection of the Law
   c. Article 2 – Freedom
   d. Article 21 – Access to Public Services

MASTERY AND ASSESSMENT OF
KNOWLEDGE OF SKILLS

Please choose the *best* answer from among the possible choices.

1. Virginia is a first-year MSW student intern at Moving Toward Maturity, which is an independent living center in a metropolitan area. In one of her substance abuse groups she makes a statement about the "universality" of drug abuse because:

    a. The problem is all-encompassing.
    b. Everyone experiences that problem at one point in his or her life.
    c. Virginia wants people in the group to relate to each other as early as possible.
    d. Her statement helps the clients feel less alone with the problem.

2. Johnny and Jon, a gay couple, come to inquire about the steps for adopting a little boy at Solid Families, a family service adoption agency. It is known by many at Solid Families that you are homophobic and you are the next social worker in rotation. In your discussion with Johnny and Jon, you learn that their inability to have children and other unmet needs regarding a family has led to relational problems between Johnny and Jon. The next step the social worker should do is:

    a. Refuse to provide them with information regarding the steps for adoption.
    b. Take the adoptive application and tell them that you will call them at some point in the future.
    c. Take the application and suggest they may need relationship counseling.
    d. Strongly insist on a diagnostic evaluation and referral for relationship counseling.

3. Keisha, an African American MSW student, is in her second semester of her first year at Families Now, a family counseling agency. She has noticed that her supervisor, Sandy, who is white, has been assigning less-skilled counselors who provide lower-quality services to areas of the community that contain more at-risk populations of color. Sandy's actions are more associated with:

    a. Individual racism
    b. Institutional racism
    c. Discrimination
    d. Aversive racism

4. Francisco is a social work intern at the local community health center located in a predominantly Hispanic community that is known for its high rate of prostitution and crime. There has also been an increase in the reports of undocumented residents in the past six months. Francisco

has been asked to brainstorm with his supervisor and director of the program on steps to take regarding the best strategy that will result in the greatest success. Francisco should:

a. Offer outreach medical services.
b. Advertise in local ethnic newspapers.
c. Contract with some of the Latino residents to visit community members, do case finding, and reassure the community that the service maintains client confidentiality, and will not reveal people's identity or immigration status.
d. Ask local schools to refer people for health services.

5. J. J., a six-year-old African American male, has been tested by the elementary school's district psychologist, Dr. White. The tests reveal a learning disability of which his parents disagree and have discussed their concerns with Lavonne, the school social worker. They argue that they have a prior right to choose the kind of education that shall be given to J. J. and that they are concerned because of past allegations of aversive racism by parents about Dr. White. Lastly, they express their concerns because of rumors of stereotyping by Dr. White toward other children of color in the school district. The best suggestion that Lavonne should provide for the family is to:

a. Work through their denial and accept the results of the test.
b. Recommend that the mother spend less time on her job and more time helping J. J. with his homework.
c. Suggest that they have J. J. tested by a psychologist of their choice.
d. Recommend that Dr. White retest J. J. and be culturally sensitive because of past rumors and allegations.

6. Larry is a first-year student at Helping Hands Housing, a social agency with a mission to assist with access to housing for populations at risk for discrimination. Larry learns that the manager of a new apartment complex has refused to rent to several of his gay and lesbian clients even after they have met all of the requirements. Larry has been instructed by his supervisor to suggest a plan of action to assist in this situation. The best strategy Larry might adopt is to:

a. Suggest that the families affected by the manager's refusal to rent to them sue the manager for damages.
b. Research the existing antidiscrimination statutes and institutions and contact the corporate office in an effort to inform them of the manager's actions and force the apartment complex to comply with the law.
c. Publicize the apartment complex behavior in the local news.
d. Suggest that his clients contact their friends and organize a "sit-in" in protest of the apartment.

7. Milton is in his second semester of his foundation internship at the local Community Services Board (CSB). Sal Lee and Alli Lee are Asian immigrants who have recently moved to the community and have been assigned to Milton's caseload. Milton has learned that the CSB has historically struggled with assisting those in the Asian community, and is concerned about developing better strategies to help the Lee family in particular and the Asian community in general to understand and embrace the services CSB provides. This can be made possible most promptly by:

   a. Improving the level of education for both the Lees and the Asian community in their area.
   b. Planning outreach efforts to approach Asian families.
   c. Making available bilingual, bicultural, and culturally competent staff who can create a climate of acceptance.
   d. Enhancing the family's ability to utilize the Western health and social services system.

8. Moving Toward Maturity (MTM) has been serving the community for over 40 years with independent living services. It is a transitional living program that provides residential and vocational training programs for at-risk adolescents ages 17 to 21. Although the composition of the community has changed to reflect that of more racial, ethnic, and religious diversity, the executive director, upper administration, and staff are still predominately male, middle class, and Anglo-Saxon. MTM is accustomed to being entrenched in the community; nevertheless it has noticed a dramatic decline in referrals and is considering downsizing for economic reasons. What fair and equitable steps should the executive director first employ?

   a. Retire and hire an executive director who is from the most prominent racial ethnic groups in the community.
   b. Replace the director and hire a Hispanic female.
   c. Systematically appraise Moving Toward Maturity's mission, staffing patterns, and programs with the involvement of an outside consultant.
   d. Attend several of the mosques, synagogues, and houses of worship and share his vision for the community.

9. John, a recent graduate of an MSW program, has been contracted as a consultant to assist Moving Toward Maturity with their challenge in lieu of downsizing. What steps should John first take in response to the problem?

   a. Suggest that the executive director replace the director and some of the staff with more people of diversity.
   b. Suggest that the executive director retire and be replaced by a person of color.

   c. Suggest that the executive director change their name, re-staff, and hire more women, people of color, and non-Christians.

   d. Review the mission, vision, and goals of Moving Toward Maturity; conduct a needs assessment from the staff; and collaborate with local colleges and universities that support diversity.

10. Jimmy, a student from the local Historical Black College and University (HBCU), is a first-semester MSW student intern at Moving Toward Maturity. He is from the community and very familiar with the challenges that MTM has faced over the years due to their lack of culturally competent clinicians. Jimmy has been shadowing Mark, a white social worker, at MTM most of the semester. He has noticed that Mark appears to be very uncomfortable, disingenuous, and unable to connect with clients of another race, ethnic group, or sexual orientation. Jimmy should suggest to Mark to:

   a. Ask that clients that make him feel uncomfortable be transferred to a social worker within the clients' race, ethnic group, or sexual orientation.

   b. Actively seek knowledge, be as genuine as possible, and try to connect on some level with the client.

   c. Change nothing, because by trial and error he will eventually learn how to better communicate and therefore will feel better and more comfortable.

   d. Expect the clients to teach him more about their diversity.

11. MTM has reviewed their mission and vision and plans to expand their services to include physically disabled and mentally ill youth. Their plan is to open a group home in a well-known middle class neighborhood, but the neighbors oppose the idea. Jimmy the social work intern has been asked to spearhead the efforts. He should do all of the following *except*:

   a. Schedule a meeting with the county board and advocate for this population.

   b. Research the existing antidiscrimination statutes and human rights laws and advocate for fair housing for this at-risk population.

   c. Extend an open door policy for all of the neighbors once the agency is allowed in the neighborhood.

   d. Change the current plans and look for another location.

Questions 12 to 15 are based on the following paragraph:

Yvette is an Asian American first-year student in her second semester as a school social worker. The high school is a predominately white high school located in an affluent area in a rural community. She has met several times with Alonzo, an African American transfer student from an inner-city school in a metropolitan area. Alonzo has transitioned well as a minority into a majority environment and has proven to be a good student with excellent communication skills. Alonzo has expressed concerns that he feels that he is not being treated fairly by one of his teachers, although has good grades and is a candidate for the school's honor society. He further explains that he feels that his history teacher, Ms. Smith, ignores him whenever he raises his hand, and that when she was his homeroom teacher, not once did she call on him the entire quarter. Alonzo shared that he had discussed his concerns with his mother and she asked him not to say anything that would jeopardize his chances of getting a good education. He further explained that he had spoken with the assistant principal when he noticed her treatment of him during homeroom in the subsequent quarter; however, no corrective actions were taken. Ms. Smith has been teaching for 35 years, all of which has been spent at the same high school, and she refuses to "pay any attention" to the rules and regulations.

12. The first step that Yvette, the student social worker, should take is to:

   a. Explore Ms. Smith's resistance to respecting Alonzo's human rights.
   b. Develop a plan of action to protect Alonzo's human rights.
   c. Discuss her concerns regarding Alonzo and Ms. Smith during weekly supervision.
   d. Speak with the assistant principal and inquire why she hasn't taken any corrective actions to protect Alonzo's human rights such as access to education.

13. When Yvette meets with Ms. Smith, she should explore her thoughts and feelings concerning:

   a. Racism
   b. Ethics
   c. Economic deprivation
   d. Populations at risk

14. When the social work intern meets with Alonzo's mother, she may discuss all but:

   a. That education shall be directed to the full development of the human personality and to the strengthening of respect for human rights and fundamental freedoms. It shall promote understanding, tolerance, and friendship among all racial or religious groups.
   b. That Ms. Smith is an old racist and will probably never change.
   c. That a parent has a right to choose the kind of education that shall be given to her child.
   d. That Alonzo's rights were violated because of Ms. Smith's prejudgment and negative treatment of him based on his race.

15. When Yvette meets with Alonzo, she should:

    a. Explain that breaking the cycle of oppression involves active reflections, confrontation, and transcendence.
    b. Suggest that he move back to his the inner-city school to be around "his" people.
    c. Discuss his feelings regarding his unfair treatment by Ms. Smith and the lack of action by the assistant principal as well as his mother's advice to remain silent.
    d. Share her personal views with him regarding her experiences with oppression, prejudice, and racism.

Reflective Essay Questions

1. Discuss the relationship between the Universal Declaration of Human Rights and the National Association of Social Workers Code of ethics regarding human rights and social justice.

2. Discuss Article 17 – Access to Housing and Article 25 – Access to Adequate Standard of Living including Healthcare as defined in the Universal Declaration of Human Rights and its relationship to social work and your client base.

3. Discuss the term "oppression" and provide an example that you have observed or experienced either in social work or elsewhere.

4. Define and describe the various forms of racism and provide examples of these definitions from your experience both personally and educationally.

5. Discuss some of the global interconnections of oppression, discrimination and institutional inequalities.

6

RESEARCH BASED
PRACTICE

DETAILED UNDERSTANDING
AND EXPLANATION (DUE)

While personal intuition and "sixth sense" are important abilities to have and, at times, can prove to be accurate, the field of social work no longer functions just on "gut" feelings and undocumented outcomes. Research-based practice is an essential addition to the evolution of the practice of social work, and will be the basis of your learning in your foundation year. Research can be seen as the process of systematically gaining information, assimilating knowledge, and gathering data in a logical manner in an effort to become informed about something; or simply, research is an organized study that adds to or verifies existing knowledge (Faulkner & Faulkner, 2009). The purpose of research in social work is to answer questions, acquire new knowledge, and learn better practice methods that will help clients. Practice evaluation and the utilization of research are important skills you will begin to learn during your foundation year. This includes learning the different methods of collecting data, data analysis, and applying the knowledge gained from your research to design interventions for your clients in addition to learning methods to assess your clinical effectiveness. Research is an important component of your learning in your foundation year because it is in your first year of coursework that you discover the correlation between practice and science and learn the steps on how to "engage in research-informed practice and obtain the needed tools to practice-informed research" (CSWE, 2008). You will also begin to integrate "learned research" with "applied research" in your field placements. Social work research connects a systematic quest for knowledge with a planned procedure that utilizes specific methodology for the study of research hypotheses and questions derived from theory or practice. The progress of the social work profession depends on the contributions made by organized and planned research and is the basis of scientific progress.

In your foundation year, you will learn the research process along with commonly used terminologies and research designs. This will help you identify with the political, ethical, and value issues at different stages in the research process. Gaining an understanding of the research process and the procedures used to protect the population that you will be studying will be very beneficial once you have identified a population that you are passionate about and desire to serve. As a social work student, you will begin to understand the association between human diversity and the research process. You will also begin to learn the relevance of your field practice experiences and the implications its interpretation has on the development of your research skills. Research skills such as (1) conceptualizing a problem; (2) formulating hypotheses and objectives; (3) designing research strategy; (4) collecting, analyzing, and interpreting both quantitative and qualitative data; including (5) frequently encountered statistical procedures are areas in research that you will learn in your first year that will be the basis of your understanding and appreciation of social work research. Because of the enormity and importance of research-based practice, this section of the workbook will briefly touch on some of the key principles, such as the research process, terminology, design, and measurements. The latter part of this chapter will also briefly discuss the importance and relevance of ethical principles in social work research, such as the IRB process, voluntary participation consent forms, anonymity, and confidentiality.

The research process and methods of data collection are very important procedures that you will learn during your first year. The research process is a method of accumulating knowledge that involves many separate steps. The number of steps in this process may vary depending on your professor; however, they generally include the following: (1) identifying a problem, (2) defining that problem in terms of a question that is capable of study, (3) developing a plan to answer the question, (4) gathering data according to prescribed practice, and (5) drawing conclusions from the data (Krysik & Finn, 2010, p. 48). There are two fields of research or methods of data collection that you will learn during your foundation year: qualitative and quantitative study.

Patten (2002) identifies qualitative study as an approach in social research based on observations made in the field and analyzed in nonstatistical ways, in which data collection is done in an unstructured manner. For example, if you were to use an unstructured interview, the end result would be in the form of qualitative data. If you ask your subjects to keep a journal of what they are doing or how their attitudes are affected as a result of a longitudinal study, the data would also be qualitative data (Patten, 2002). At the extreme end of the qualitative approach is the belief that the only truly viable form of data collection is through open, unstructured methods (Dooley, 2001).

In quantitative study or research, the aim is to determine the relationship between one thing (an independent variable) and another (a dependent or outcome variable) in a population. Quantitative research designs are either descriptive (subjects usually measured once) or experimental (subjects measured before and after a treatment). A descriptive study establishes only associations between variables. An experiment establishes causality. Simply put, quantitative study research results are presented as quantities or numbers. In a quantitative study, a researcher emphasizes instruments or measuring tools that produce data that can quickly be reduced to numbers, such as structured questionnaires or interview schedules with objective formats such as multiple-choice questions (Berg, 2009; Dooley, 2001; Patten, 2002).

In order to continue the process of building a solid research foundation, there are a number of research terms that you will become familiar with in your first year. Some of the terms will require that you develop an understanding as early as possible in your first year in your MSW program, and are briefly discussed in this section of the workbook. These terms include but are not limited to the following: theory, hypothesis, independent variable, dependent variable, operationalizing, and conceptualization.

Theory is a "way of organizing facts or sets of facts to describe, explain, or predict events." In other words, it is a statement or set of statements designed to explain a phenomenon based upon observation generally agreed upon by most experts in a particular field (Ambrosino, Heffernan, Shuttlesworth, & Ambrosino, 2008, p. 52; Faulkner & Faulkner, 2009). Your understanding of theory will help during the various stages of planning, implementing, and evaluating an intervention, as well as help to shape the pursuit of answers to why, what, and how questions. For example, theory can be used to guide the search for reasons why some HIV-positive youth are not following public health and medical advice and are not caring for themselves in healthy ways. Your understanding of theory can help pinpoint what you need to know before developing or organizing an intervention program, and provide insight into how to shape program strategies to reach youth and organizations and make an impact on them. Lastly, theory also helps identify what should be monitored, measured, and/or compared with regard to the intervention (Neuman & Wiegand, 2000; Dooley, 2001).

Hypothesis, dependent variables, and independent variables are very important terms for you to grasp in your first research course. Hypothesis consists of a prediction about the relations among operational terms or variables, usually drawn by deduction from a theory. In its simplest form, a hypothesis is a prediction of the outcome of a study that may be based on an educated guess or a formal theory. You can also have a null hypothesis, which is a prediction of an outcome contrary to what is expected that serves as the rival hypothesis tested by inferential statistics (Dooley, 2001). Variables are characteristics or properties that can vary or take on different values or attributes (Schutt, 2006, p. 71). An independent variable is a characteristic or property that causes or produces the effect in a causal explanation—for example, time, social class, income, inequality, race/ethnicity, or families. A dependent variable is any variable in research that defines separate groups of subjects on which the dependent measure is taken. Subjects may be assigned to these groups on the basis of either (1) some preexisting characteristics (differential research), such as HIV-positive status or higher-risk negatives; or (2) some form of random assignment (experimental research) (Dooley, 2001). In other words, the dependent variable is the variable that is changed or predicted by another variable or is said to depend on the other variable (independent variable).

In your foundation research courses, you will have assigned research projects in which you will have to review literature on certain social problems or societal ills and will study topics that challenge social conditions or social policies. Two questions that you will ask yourself at the onset of your research will entail you having a solid understanding of conceptualization and operationalization. For example, "What is meant by 'child abuse' in this research?" (the conceptualization issue) and "How is child abuse measured?" (the operationalization issue). Each question must be answered when reviewing previous research on child abuse and must be considered when designing new research (Schutt, 2006; Rubin & Babbie, 2008; Patten, 2002).

Conceptualization is the process of taking a construct or concept and refining it by giving it a conceptual or theoretical definition. Ordinary dictionary definitions will not do. Instead, you must take keywords in your research question or hypothesis and find a clear and consistent definition that is agreed upon by scholars in the scientific community. Conceptualization is often guided by the theoretical framework, perspective, or approach the researcher is committed to (Miller, 1991; Faulkner & Faulkner, 2009; Engel & Schutt, 2009). Operationalizing in research is the explanation of the phenomenon or observable fact to be studied in terms of how it will be measured. To operationalize a concept means to define it in a measurable way. Operationalizing a concept provides conceptual clarity and removes all ambiguity about the meaning of the concept. In this process, you can draw on prior research to help identify the options for operationalizing a concept (Krysik & Finn, 2010; Dooley, 2001; Patten, 2002). For example, a social work researcher may wish to measure "anger." Simply put, operationalizing is redefining a variable in terms of physical steps. It is perfectly acceptable in science to borrow the conceptualizations and operationalizations of others.

During your first year, you will begin to understand the inherent problems in some research designs and their production. You will begin to secure a basic understanding of the use of descriptive research, correlational studies, cross-sectional studies, and developmental studies in interpreting and evaluating research. Descriptive research identifies characteristics of an observed phenomenon; explores possible correlations among two or more phenomena; and describes a situation as it is, without manipulation. Descriptive research types are correlational studies, developmental studies, observational studies, and survey studies. (Dooley, 2001; Rubin & Babbie, 2008; Marczyk et al., 2005). Very simple types of statistics are used in descriptive research, such as mean, median, mode, standard deviation, percentage (chi-square test), and sometimes correlation. Correlational studies examine the extent to which differences in one characteristic or variable are related to differences in one or more other characteristics or variables. They do not indicate causation and are dependent upon the reliability and validity of the measurement instrument. Developmental studies are cross-sectional, meaning people from different age groups are sampled and compared; and are also longitudinal, meaning a single group of people is followed for months or years (Dooley, 2001; Miller, 1991; Patten, 2002). Problems with cross-sectional studies are that the subjects have inherent differences (upbringing, societal changes, etc.) that contaminate some comparisons. Correlations cannot be made between characteristics at different age levels. Problems with longitudinal studies are that they are more difficult and time-consuming, and respondents can develop a familiarity with a measurement instrument that precludes accurate and truthful responses (Miller, 1991).

You will learn about exploratory, explanatory, and experimental research that will help support your evidence-based interventions and research findings to evaluate your practice. Exploratory research is data collection and analysis aimed at formulation of hypotheses, and seeks to build theory rather than test it. As the term suggests, exploratory research is often conducted because a problem has not been clearly defined as yet, or its real scope is as yet unclear. It can also fill in the gaps in existing theory and is generally used for any research with small and/or poor samples. Exploratory research is also designed to define ranges and develop clues or hunches that will help to establish a hypothesis. It is desirable in exploratory research to conduct at least two group sessions on a project, but frequently not more than one group with any one narrow segment of the population involved. The findings and interpretations from the group or groups in exploratory research are likely to be about the same by all unbiased analysis, meaning the ranges are established, direction identified, and hypotheses generated. Exploratory research helps determine the best research design, data collection method, and selection of subjects. Explanatory research focuses on why events occur or it tries to test and build social theory (Tukey, 1977; Rubin & Babbie, 2008; Schutt, 2006).

Experimental research is a methodical way of comparing two or more groups to determine differences in the effect of different treatments received by each group. In experimental research, the researcher purposely manipulates a treatment (independent variable) to see if it causes a change in the effect (dependent variable). In experimental research, experimental design is a blueprint of the procedure that enables the researcher to test the hypothesis by reaching valid conclusions about relationships between independent and dependent variables (Patten, 2002). Experimental research, therefore, becomes the conceptual framework within which the experiment is conducted, in which a treatment can be an educational program, new drug, or procedure that is being tested for its "effect" on the dependent variable such as knowledge, attitude, belief, and behavior of prevention programs regarding HIV/AIDS (Miller, 1991; Rubin & Babbie, 2008; Schutt, 2006).

In your foundation year, you will begin to understand the importance of measurements in research, particularly when evaluating the success of the programs at your field placements. You will learn to use your research findings to improve practice behaviors at your practicum sites, develop and/or reform policy within the agencies that you intern, and deliver improved evidence-based social services to your client base. An understanding of the levels of measurement, measurement validity, and reliability will all assist you with ways of understanding during your foundation year. Dooley (2001) defines reliability as an index of the consistency of a measuring instrument in repeatedly providing the same score for a given subject. Reliability refers to the degree to which observed scores are "free from errors of measurement" (Dooley, 2001). Although unreliability is always present to a certain extent, there will generally be a good deal of consistency in the results of a quality instrument gathered at different times. The tendency toward consistency found in repeated measurements is referred to as reliability (Patten, 2002). Validity refers to the appropriateness, meaningfulness, and usefulness of specific inferences made from the measures and belongs not just to a measure but depends on the fit between the measure and its label. It can be defined as the degree to which a test measures what it is supposed to measure. There are three basic approaches to the validity of tests and measures. Any measuring device is valid if it, in fact, measures what it purports to measure. A self-esteem scale is valid if it measures self-esteem and not something else, such as "narcissism" (Dooley, 2001).

You will learn the significance of scientific and ethical approaches to building knowledge in social work research and its impact on your field placement experience and ultimately your postgraduate practice. You will discover, in your research course, ethical principles outlined by the Belmont report that guide ethical decision making in research. You will find that your adherence to and support of these ethical principles will come easier after a review of history that involved horrific acts and inhumane treatment, such as the Nazi atrocities and the Tuskegee Syphilis Study in Alabama. Furthermore, you will learn the ethical guidelines for social work research as they relate to the importance of IRB process, the value of voluntary participation, the need for consent forms, and the requirements of anonymity and confidentiality.

Just as the practice of social work deals with people and problems, so does the research of social work. In order to carry out a research-based practice supported by evidenced-based interventions, you must clearly understand the ethical principles that protect your clients. Every scientific investigation has an ethical component to it, especially in social work research, since it oftentimes confronts distinctive ethical challenges. Because of past abuse in research, Congress established the National Research Act, which created the Belmont Report, which outlined three ethical principles that should guide ethical decision making in research: (1) respect for the individual, (2) beneficence, and (3) justice. Respect for the person implies that a person should be treated as an autonomous individual, capable of making informed decisions when provided the information to do so. It also gives consideration for vulnerable populations such as the aged, disabled, and minorities. The principle of beneficence simply is minimizing possible harms and maximizing benefits, while justice is distributing benefits and risk of research fairly (Krysik & Finn, 2010; Faulkner & Faulkner, 2009).

An institutional review board (IRB) is a peer/community review committee of five or more individuals who volunteer their time to review research proposals and monitor ongoing research studies to ensure that people (often referred to as human subjects) participating in research are being adequately protected. IRBs may be associated with an academic institution, a hospital, or an employing or contracting agency or organization (Krysik & Finn, 2010, p. 35). The voluntary participation of human subjects means that they are aware that they are participating in a study and are informed of all the consequences of the study and consent to participate in the study. The consent form is a form that human subjects sign before participating in a study, which provides full information about the features of the study that might affect their decision about whether to participate, particularly regarding its procedures, potential harm, and anonymity and confidentiality (Rubin & Babbie, 2008). Anonymity means that you will not collect any identifying information on the subjects participating in your research study, while confidentiality is when all information about the subjects of your research, and all answers they provide, will remain in the hands of the investigator and no person outside the research process will have access to their information. Subjects have a basic right to know that their information will be kept confidential, which also helps them self-report honestly.

Your class work, private studies, group projects, and practicum experiences will all help you in grasping the research concepts and complex terminologies as well as the application of research methods. Research is all around you and you use it every day and in every aspect of your social world. When you surf the Internet or check your social network account, you are conducting research. Many negative and self-defeating thoughts might enter your mind regarding research in social work and you might not see the importance of it, particularly if you desire to be a clinician. You might also associate success in research with the mastery of mathematics and statistics. You might even think that securing a solid foundation in research is only for the very intelligent. If any of those are your concerns, do not be worried: you are not alone. Many have approached the study of research with anxiety and apprehension. At some point in your foundation year, you will marvel at your ability to evaluate the quality and relevance of research studies as you are able to communicate the basic language, concepts, and principles of both qualitative and quantitative social research. You will marvel at your ability to identify and formulate problems in social welfare that are amenable to research, and at your ability to analyze and communicate research methods in writing. You will be amazed at your understanding of the relationship between research, human behavior, practice, and other areas of social work knowledge; all of which you will experience during your foundation year.

UNDERSTANDING OF KNOWLEDGE

Please choose the *best* answer from among the possible choices.

1. Research is defined as all of the following *except*:

   a. The systematic procedures used in seeking facts or principles
   b. The process of systematically gaining information, assimilating knowledge, and gathering data in a logical manner in an effort to become informed about something
   c. Knowledge of poverty, marginalization, alienation, privilege, and power
   d. A systematic study that adds to or verifies existing knowledge

2. To answer questions and acquire a new knowledge base while improving practice methods that will help clients, and to connect in a systematic quest for knowledge with a planned procedure that utilizes specific methodology for the study of research hypotheses and questions derived from theory or practice, are the *purpose* and *result* of:

   a. Social justice
   b. Social work research
   c. Economic deprivation
   d. Ethics

3. All of the following are basic research skills that you will learn during your foundation year, *except*:

   a. Conceptualizing a problem and designing research strategy
   b. Formulating hypotheses and objectives
   c. Creating the problem and social constructs that prevent the solution to the problem
   d. Collecting, analyzing, and interpreting both quantitative and qualitative data, including frequently encountered statistical procedures

4. The two fields of research or methods of data collection discussed in this chapter that you will learn about during your foundation year are:

   a. Qualitative and quantitative
   b. Independent and dependent
   c. Anonymity and confidentiality
   d. Operationalization and conceptualization

5. The steps in the research process include:

    a. Recognizing a problem; defining that problem; developing a plan to answer the question; gathering data according to prescribed practice; and answering the problem to the betterment of your client base
    b. Identifying a problem; defining that problem in terms of a question that is capable of study; providing resources to fund the problem; gathering data according to prescribed practice; and drawing conclusions from the data
    c. Identifying a problem; defining that problem in terms of a question that is capable of study; developing a plan to answer the question; gathering data according to prescribed practice; and drawing conclusions from the data
    d. Identifying a problem; defining that problem in terms of a question that is capable of study; developing a plan to answer the question; gathering data according to prescribed practice; and drawing conclusions from the data and then publishing them

6. An approach in social research based on observations made in the field and analyzed in nonstatistical ways, in which data collection is done in an unstructured manner, is called a:

    a. Cross-sectional study
    b. Qualitative study
    c. Correlational study
    d. Quantitative study

7. A group of related hypotheses, concepts, and constructs, based on facts and observations, that attempts to explain a particular phenomenon is best known as:

    a. Dependent variable
    b. Theory
    c. Variable
    d. Operationalization

8. The process of taking a construct or concept and refining it by giving it a conceptual or theoretical definition is best known as:

    a. Operationalizing
    b. Exploration
    c. Conceptualization
    d. Explanation

9. All of the following are accurate about exploratory research *except*:

   a. It is data collection and analysis aimed at formulation of hypotheses and seeks to build theory rather than test it.
   b. It is often conducted because a problem has not been clearly defined as yet, or its real scope is as yet unclear.
   c. It focuses on why events occur or it tries to test and build social theory.
   d. It is also designed to define ranges and develop clues or hunches that will help to establish a hypothesis.

10. This is a research study that is either descriptive (subjects usually measured once) or experimental (subjects measured before and after a treatment); established associations between variables and research results are presented as quantities or numbers.

    a. Cross-sectional study
    b. Qualitative study
    c. Correlational study
    d. Quantitative study

11. A peer/community review committee of five or more individuals who volunteer their time to review research proposals and monitor ongoing research studies to ensure that people (often referred to as human subjects) participating in research are being adequately protected refers to:

    a. IRB – Instructional Review Board
    b. IRB – Institutional Review Board
    c. NASW – National Association of Social Workers
    d. CSWE – Council on Social Work Education

12. The three principles outlined in the Belmont Report that should guide ethical decision making in research are:

    a. Respect for the individual, beneficence, and justice
    b. Anonymity, confidentiality, and ethics
    c. Reliability, validity, and variables
    d. Strong focus on community, adaptability of family roles, and a strong religious belief system

13. This refers to the appropriateness, meaningfulness, and usefulness of specific inferences made from the measures and belongs not just to a measure but depends on the fit between the measure and its label, and can be defined as the degree to which a test measures what it is supposed to measure.

    a. Reliability   c. Variables
    b. Validity   d. Measurements

14. Anonymity is best defined as:

   a. Not collecting any identifying information on the subjects participating in your research study.
   b. Assuring the human subjects of your research that all information about them, and all answers they provide, will remain in the hands of the investigator and that no person outside the research process will have access to their information.
   c. Insuring that human subjects are aware that they are participating in a study and are informed of all the consequences of the study and consent to participate in the study.
   d. Asking human subjects to sign a form before participating in a study that provides full information about the features of the study that might affect their decision about whether to participate, particularly regarding its procedures and potential harm.

15. A characteristic or property that can vary or take on different values or attributes is best known in research as a:

   a. Theory
   b. Variable
   c. Construct
   d. Concept

MASTERY AND ASSESSMENT OF KNOWLEDGE OF SKILLS

Please choose the *best* answer from among the possible choices.

1. John, an MSW intern, is a social worker at a local high school. He is interested in the reliability of a questionnaire regarding safe-sex practices. The best method to check the reliability of his survey is to:

   a. Ask the first-period sex education students to complete the questionnaire and then administer the same questionnaire to the second-period sex education students.
   b. Ask the first-period sex education students to complete the questionnaire and then administer the same questionnaire to them again.
   c. Ask the first-period sex education students to complete the questionnaire and then administer the questionnaire to them again, but add additional questions that require more thinking.
   d. Ask the first-period sex education students to complete the questionnaire and then administer the same questionnaire to a first-period sex education class at another high school.

2. When the instructor in a social work class asks students to fill out a questionnaire that he or she hopes to analyze and publish, students should always be told their participation in the survey is completely voluntary. Even so, most students will fear that nonparticipation will somehow affect their grade. The instructor should do all of the following *except*:

   a. Be especially sensitive to such belief in implied sanctions and make special previsions to obviate them.
   b. Leave the room while the questionnaires are being completed.
   c. Ask the students to return the questionnaires by mail or drop them in a box near the door just before the next course meeting.
   d. Leave the room but ask the students to place their student identification in the left side of the last page of the questionnaire.

3. You are designing an exploratory study in which you will collect information on how clients feel about the services in your agency. All of the following are steps you should take that will allow the individuals to remain anonymous *except*:

   a. Ask the clients to place responses in a comment box in the lobby or waiting room.
   b. Ask the clients to write comments on a blank piece of paper and give them to the receptionist to place in an unmarked envelope.
   c. Ask the clients to e-mail, text, or respond via the office Facebook account.
   d. Ask the clients to mail in their concerns and provide them with a self-addressed stamped envelope.

4. You are designing an exploratory study at your field placement in which you will collect information on how clients feel about the services in your agency. However, you notice that only clients with complaints are making use of the comment box. In your weekly meeting with your agency supervisor you discuss your concern and you both decide to change from the exploratory study to a descriptive study for which you develop a form that allows clients to rate their satisfaction with various services on a scale from 1 to 10. To maintain anonymity for your clients, you should do all of the following *except*:

   a. Invite all clients to complete the form and do not ask for any information that can be used to identify the clients, such as name, age, occupation, or client file number.
   b. Provide all clients checking into your agency with the form and ask them to complete it before leaving and place it in the comment box.
   c. Invite all clients who came in the office to complete the form and not put their name or any identifying information on it, and then give them an option to mail it in or bring it back at their next appointment time.
   d. Ask the clients to complete the form with no identifying information, and then you place them in their client files for future review.

5. You are conducting a quantitative study on caregiver burnout for persons living with HIV/AIDS. You have explained the study, answered all questions by the participants, and gotten the consent forms signed. As you are beginning the study, you become aware that one of the participants appears uncomfortable and has stopped answering the questionnaire. You should:

   a. Ask the participant if there is a problem, address his concerns, and encourage him to continue with the study since you have his signed consent to participate.

   b. Ignore the participant because your role is that of a researcher and not a counselor and you already have a signed consent where he agreed to participate.

   c. Ask the participant if there is a problem, and if he is no longer interested in participating in the study, take up the questionnaire and allow him to leave.

   d. Share with the participant the value he adds to the body of knowledge regarding caregiver burnout and schedule a future session with him to address his concerns.

6. LaNorris, a biracial first-year MSW student, is conducting a qualitative research study on race relations at a predominantly white institution, and begins the one-on-one key informant interviews after the consent forms have been signed. During the interview one participant begins to respond to questions asked with racial epithets in referring to a teacher of color at the school. The best steps LaNorris should take are to:

   a. Stop the interview and share with the key informant that he is biracial.

   b. Continue with the questions and key informant interview, but speak with the participant about human dignity and the worth of others.

   c. Complete the questions and the key informant interview and analyze the data.

   d. Make him feel comfortable by agreeing with him so long as he continues being honest during the interview.

7. E. J. is a social work student in his second semester of his first year in an MSW program at a large university. He is very interested in policy and plans to participate in some political advocacy with his agency. He would do all of the following *except*:

   a. Lobby for new legislation without first becoming familiar with the problem that the proposed legislation is intended to alleviate.

   b. Identify the problem the proposed legislation is intended to alleviate.

   c. Define that problem in terms of a question that the proposed legislation is intended to alleviate.

   d. Gather data according to prescribed practice that the proposed legislation is intended to alleviate.

8. The following would be a subtle violation of ethics in social work research:

   a. Because of time constraints, the social work student asks the participants to sign the consent form after the study has begun
   b. The 1932 Tuskegee Study in Alabama
   c. The language on the consent forms are beyond the educational level or understanding of the participants
   d. The Holocaust in World War II

9. Dale is a community social work student concerned about the recent increase in accidents near a busy intersection where his two boys attend school. He contacts his friend Ryan, a state patrol officer, and gets information about the 3M Driver Feedback Sign with the MUTCD RS-1 sign specifications and places one near the intersection to record the speed of every passing vehicle. He does this as part of an effort to convince the city to erect a traffic light. In this situation Dale would:

   a. Need all participants to verbally agree to be part of the study.
   b. Not need to obtain informed consent from the drivers of every automobile it observes passing through the intersection.
   c. Need to ensure that all are aware that they are participating in a study.
   d. Must inform all of the participants of the consequences of the study.

10. A. J. is a social work intern at To Better Your Life Counseling. A. J. has been asked to write a proposal for a new social program that will address the human trafficking concerns in Cobb County. The order of the research process that A. J. must endorse is to:

   a. Conduct an assessment of need, identify the overall purpose of the program, discuss the program goals, and provide measureable statements of intent.
   b. Identify the overall purpose of the program, conduct an assessment of need, discuss the program goals, and provide measureable statements of intent.
   c. Identify the overall purpose of the program, provide measureable statements of intent, conduct an assessment of need, and discuss the program goals.
   d. Conduct an assessment of need, provide measureable statements of intent, identify the overall purpose of the program, and discuss the program goals.

Reflective Essay Questions

You are interning at I Can Help (ICH) agency, which is a homeless shelter for men. This agency has been awarded a federal grant to conduct a three-month qualitative study with a vulnerable population regarding the service utilization for HIV-positive men. The study is being conducted within a metropolitan area and you understand that ICH will be asking you to be a research assistant on the project, along with your agency field supervisor. In its advertisements, ICH shared that participation was voluntary, anonymous, and confidential. However, to encourage participation, the agency also advertised that it would provide food and a $50 stipend to all of the participants. You have had a very close immediate family member recently infected with the virus that causes AIDS and it is a very sensitive topic of which you are still very emotional, and prior to the research, you tried to avoid discussing the subject. Answer the following reflective essay questions using this information as a foundational understanding.

1. What would you do regarding your participation in the study at I Can Help agency, and why?

2. You are the research assistant for the qualitative study with ICH and learn that one of the participants is the person suspected of infecting one of your close family members. What would you do, and why? In your response, discuss the concepts of anonymity, confidentiality, and respect for the individual.

3. I Can Help (ICH) is on the final month of the research project and has two more focus groups to conduct. You have done very well in the study disassociating your personal feelings from your professional obligations and have been asked by your supervisor to facilitate the final two focus groups. You notice several recurring participants who you saw at the first focus group and believe are motivated by the food and the $50 stipend. What would you do, and why?

4. Your first cousin, whom you have not seen in over fifteen years, signs up as a participant for the study. Discuss possible emotions and feelings you might experience and explain what you would do regarding the focus group and your immediate family.

5. Discuss the issues might you encounter in attempting to gain access to your cousin outside the environment of the study.

7

HUMAN
BEHAVIOR

DETAILED UNDERSTANDING
AND EXPLANATION (DUE)

   Human behavior takes place in every region of our lives and has no respect of our race, sexual orientation, spirituality, or even socioeconomic status. Whether you are African American or Asian, male or transgendered, Christian or Muslim, middle class or a product of the "have-nots," human behavior happens. It takes place in different arrangements of physical, psychological, and social environments in which you will be confronted with biological burdens, psychological stressors, and social demands that require effective human responses. Human behavior in social work is often viewed as the adaptation of people to resources and circumstances (Ashford, Lecroy, & Lortie, 2006). You will better understand the complexities of human behavior in the context of the social environment in your foundation human behavior course during your first year in the MSW program. The basis of your understanding with regard to your clients' behavior and problem-solving ability will be rooted in strengths perspective, which will sharpen your awareness of diversity and differences. You will learn that the strengths perspective is based in the assumption that individuals, families, and communities all have the capacity for growth, change, and adaptation that must viewed through the lens of their capacities, talents, competencies, possibilities, visions, values, and hopes, however rushed and unclear these may have become through circumstance, oppression, and trauma (Rogers, 2006; Saleebey, 1996).

   Just as there are many great textbooks that discuss human behavior in the social environment, there are many viewpoints that your perspective MSW programs will have adopted and teach from relative to their human behavior in social environment (HBSE) courses. To facilitate your learning human behavior across the life course in your foundation year, a number of the HBSE courses that you will become familiar with will focus on the dimensions of human behavior from life course perspective. The life course theoretical foundation is across several disciplines and has been shaped by sociologists, anthropologists, social historians, demographers, and psychologists (Hutchinson, 2008, p. 11). From this perspective you will be able to gain a level of understanding about the vibrant varying nature of person-environment transition and become familiar with: (1) the patterns in human behavior, (2) the diversity in the life course, and (3) the unique life stories of individuals. The life course perspective looks at how "chronological age, relationships, common life transitions, and social change shape people's lives from birth to death" (Hutchinson, 2008, p. 9). To help you understand your clients' life using the life course perspective, you would look at their event history or "the sequence of significant events, experiences, and transitions in a person's life from birth to death" (Hutchinson, 2008, p. 10).

The five basic concepts of the life course perspective will further your understanding about behavior across the life cycle. They are (1) cohort, (2) transition, (3) trajectory, (4) life event, and (5) turning point. Cohort is defined as a "group of persons who were born at the same historical time and who experience particular social changes within a given culture in the same sequence and at the same age" (Hutchinson, 2008; Alwin & McCammon, 2003; Newman & Newman, 2006; Settersten, 2003). Transition is the change in roles and statuses that represents a distinct departure from prior roles and status, while trajectory is seen as the long-term pattern of stability and change that usually involves multiple transitions (Hutchinson, 2008; Elder & Kirkpatrick Johnson, 2003; Hagestad, 2003). The last two basic concepts of the life course theoretical framework, life event and turning point, will help you further solidify your foundational knowledge of human behavior across the life span during your first year. Life events are seen as the significant occurrences involving relatively abrupt changes that may produce serious and long-lasting effects, such as the death of a spouse, foreclosure, or retirement from work (Hutchinson, 2008; Settersten, 2003), whereas turning points are those life events that produce a lasting shift in the life course (Hutchinson, 2008; Rutter, 1996). The life course theoretical framework will help you identify some of the effects of racial/ cultural, ethnic, gender, and economic variables on individuals and families over the life course.

During your first year, you will learn about issues related to human behavior and the social environment that are import to understand for practice. Some of the issues will be regarding individuals and families across the life cycle, with a focus on the biological, sociological, cultural, spiritual, and psychological development and mastery from birth through adulthood. Additionally, you will view these constructs through the range of social systems in which these individuals and families live and will be studying the ways these systems promote or deter them in maintaining or achieving health and well-being. You will also discuss traditional and dominant developmental theories such as the psychological theories that include the psychodynamic and psychosocial theories, and cognitive development theories that include theories of intellectual and moral development. Included in these courses are current theories and research about the life cycle, with particular emphasis on the ways in which culture, ethnicity, and community influence and shape development. You will also come to understand how your clients belonging to groups and working within communities helps to increase their sense of identity and enhance individual self-esteem, and helps them obtain a source for social comparisons between themselves and others (Ashford, LeCroy, & Lortie, 2006).

You will come to understand the various phases of development, to include: early childhood, middle childhood, adolescence, young adulthood, middle adulthood, and older adulthood. These developmental theories will focus on cognitive and emotional development as defined by four key theorists: Sigmund Freud, Erik Erikson, Jean Piaget, and Lawrence Kohlberg. You will also be given some beginning understanding of DSM-IV-TR. This was discussed in chapter 3, "Critical Thinking," which you can reference. Remember, the DSM-IV is used by all mental health professionals and will provide you with the language you will need to interact and talk with other professionals about clients. Freud's theories have developed over time into ego psychology and object relations, which you will learn during your second year. Erikson's theories cover the entire life cycle, beginning with birth and ending with death. Piaget's four stages of development focus on cognitive development through adolescence and Kohlberg's research was an outgrowth of Piaget's work and focused on the development of moral judgment. There are many other theories and perspectives on individual development that are studied; however, these theories represent some of the most influential thinking regarding individual human behavior and development within the social work discipline.

Sigmund Freud was a physician and psychoanalyst who developed the psychoanalytic theory, which was the basis of psychodynamic theory used by social workers. Freud's stages of development are used less today because theory has expanded to ego psychology and object relations, which you will study in your second year. Freud identifies the five stages of psychosexual development as: (1) oral stage, (2) anal stage, (3) phallic stage, (4) latency stage, and (5) genital stage. His developmental stages focus on critical developmental periods and the role of sexuality in development from infancy on (Rogers, 2006; Freud, 1920). In the oral stage, birth to 18 months, focus is on the mouth and upper digestive tract as the main channels of gratification. Its pleasure centers on activities of the mouth such as feeding, sucking, chewing, and biting and the gratifying objects include nipple and its mother. The anal stage, 18 months to 3 years, is when the child gains control over his sphincter and bowels and can therefore control the elimination of waste. According to Freud, this is associated with sexual pleasure, personal power, and control. The phallic stage is the third stage, which is from 3 to 5 years. In this stage the main source of gratification shifts from the anal to the genital zone in which pleasure centers on self-manipulation (Rogers, 2006; Freud, 1920). In the next stage, you will learn how gender conflicts and defense mechanisms work. Freud argues that boys and girls deal with the Oedipus and Electra complexes. The Oedipus complex begins at about age 4, in which a boy's phallic striving is directed toward the mother and he falls in love with her and is in competition with the father for her attention. In the Electra complex, girls' development leads to repression of desire for the father and identification with the mother and internalization of her values. They struggle with penis envy, symbolic of the power of the father and male, and consequently feel inferior to boys, which is the foundation for their submissiveness and other gender roles later in life.

Freud's fourth stage, the latent stage, is from 6 to 10 years. It is characterized by the sublimation of the Oedipal stage, with the expression of sexual and aggressive drives in socially acceptable forms (Rogers, 2006; Freud, 1920). It is in this stage that sexual instincts are un-aroused and the child's focus is on play, learning, and socialization. The last stage of Freud's psychosexual development is the genital stage, age 10 to adulthood. This is where pleasure centers on love, work, and maturing sexually. It is in this stage where genitalia are accepted and concern for the well-being of others is developed. As with life, this theory is not without weaknesses and strengths. Some of the weaknesses of Freud's psychosexual development are: (1) it frequently does not seem applicable to client situations, (2) the psychoanalysis process can be very time consuming, (3) constructs in his theory are difficult to define, measure, and test, (4) it focuses only on the individual, ignoring the impact of outside forces on client problems, and (5) his ideas are said to be based on the experiences of his patients, who were almost exclusively wealthy Caucasian women. An identified strength of this theory is that it brought to the forefront sexual issues in psychological thinking (Roger, 2006).

Erik Erikson worked with Freud, and his theory of psychosocial development integrated many of the basic beliefs of the Freudian theory; however, in contrast, it assumes that people follow a sequence of stages of development from birth through death, and Erikson was interested in explaining those developments. Erik Erikson was an ego psychologist whose eight developmental stages cover the life span from birth to death and can be viewed from a strengths perspective. At each stage, the child or adult must master the specific identified tasks prior to moving to the next stage. In Erikson's first stage, infancy: trust versus mistrust (birth to 18 months), the baby expects to be nurtured and taken care of and the caregiver is expected to provide the child with nurturance and emotional support. The mutual interchange that occurs between the baby and the caregiver forms the basis for basic trust for the child. The second stage, early childhood: autonomy versus shame and doubt (18 months to 3 years), is the period when the toddler learns to walk and to achieve a certain independence over his or her own body. Walking allows the child to explore, which helps the child to gain self-confidence and pride. During this phase the child develops a sense of identity based on social experiences and demonstrates a strong willpower. This stage allows the child to begin to move away from the mother, but to see her as a source of support that he or she can return to for "emotional refueling."

Erikson's third stage, initiative versus guilt (3 to 6 years), moves the child into a period in which his or her imagination and creativity are rich. At this point, the child has language that allows him or her to express ideas and to communicate with those in the environment. During this phase the child is able to establish small goals with which he or she seeks to reach and feel a sense of mastery. This is also Freud's phallic stage. The next phase of Erikson's psychosocial stages of development is industry versus inferiority (6 to 12 years). In this stage, the child's capacity to reason deductively and to complete various tasks, which again support his or her sense of confidence and competence, is promoted. Children at this age are invested in making things and completing puzzles. They are attending school and they learn to play and work with others and of the "give and take" involved in relationships. Children in this age range are like sponges, in that they are absorbing and learning about the world around them. The next stage, adolescence: identity versus role confusion (13 to 19 years), brings on swift hormonal changes. The adolescent's reference group shifts from parents to peers. They experience struggles coming to understand and accept themselves and their peers. The key developmental milestone is a sense of personal identity.

Erikson's sixth stage, young adulthood: intimacy versus isolation (20 to 24 years), results in the child's ability to achieve intimacy in relationships and a solid sense of identity. In this stage, the adolescent learns to find love with another and to consider the feelings of others. One is able to consider sharing one's life with another person, which can lead to intimate relations, marriage, and children. The seventh stage, adulthood: generativity versus stagnation (24 to 64 years), allows adults to feel concern for future generations and to feel a sense of responsibility for guiding young people toward meeting their goal. The final stage, old age: ego integrity versus despair (65 to death), provides the individual with wisdom and allows him or her to accept that death is inevitable. In this phase the person is able to integrate all aspects of his or her life, which allows him or her to accept death (Erikson, 1963). By and large, Erikson's eight stages of psychosocial development explain the interpenetration of biological, cultural, and psychological factors that you will study during your foundation year.

Jean Piaget was formally trained as a biologist, and his biological perspective influenced his ultimate work in cognitive psychology. He built his career on studying the relationship between how we develop and how we learn, and much of his theories of cognition were developed by closely observing his own children. Piaget's stages of cognitive development include four periods of thinking: (1) sensorimotor, (2) preoperational, (3) concrete operational, and (4) formal operational thought. In the first period, sensorimotor stage (1 to 18 months), the infant lacks symbolic function, but is able to interact with surroundings plus focus on objects other than self and learns to anticipate that events such as crying will get the attention of parents. In his second stage, the preoperational period (2 to 7 years), you see the emergence of symbolic thought derived from sensorimotor thinking; however, conceptual ability is not yet developed (Hutchison, 2008; Hudson, 2010). In other words, the child learns to use signs and symbols to think about and do things with objects and events that are absent.

In Piaget's third period, the concrete operational state (7 to 11 years), the child acquires the capacity to order and relate experiences to an organized whole and can explore several possible solutions to a problem without necessarily adopting one and is able to return to the original outlook (Ashford, LeCroy, & Lortie, 2006). The child uses logic and learns about reality by manipulating the objects of his perception mentally. It is a shift from action to thought. The child is able to represent experiences mentally, which supports language development. Language development allows the child to organize experiences mentally. It is in this stage that the child begins to reason correctly about concrete things and events with coherent and integrated cognitive systems. Piaget's final period, the formal operational stage (11 years through adolescence), is when the child visualizes events and concepts beyond the present and forms theories in which cognitive random behavior is replaced by a systematic approach to problems (Ashford, LeCroy, & Lortie, 2006). The youth gains objectivity and awareness of relative relationships, ability to reason by hypothesis and to relate past, present, and future.

Lawrence Kohlberg's moral development theory is a construct of Piaget's research that you will discuss in your foundation year. Kohlberg defines moral development as a process that takes an extended period of time and is categorized in three levels, six distinct stages, and processes from simple rewards and punishment to behavior based on moral principles concerned with the common good (Rogers, 2006; Kohlberg, 1981). He argues that children's experiences shape their understanding of moral concepts such as justice, rights, equality, and human welfare and identifies the three general levels of moral development as the preconventional, conventional, and postconventional. The preconventional level, also known as the primitive level, is where moral judgments are concrete and framed from an individual perspective that emphasizes following rules because rule-breaking may lead to punishment. The conventional level is characterized by a member-of-society perspective, while the postconventional or principled level is where ethical reasoning is formed on the basis of general principles and is understood in accordance with underlying rules and norms. This level rejects uniform application of rules or norms and is rooted in the ethical fairness principles from which moral laws are created.

Kohlberg's six stages are distributed across these three levels of judgment. "Stage 1 is characterized by a punishment-and-obedience orientation. Stage 2 is characterized by hedonism. Stage 3 focus is on maintaining good relations and the approval of others. Stage 4 focuses on conformity to social norms. Stage 5 is characterized by a sense of shared rights and duties as grounded in an implied social contract. Lastly, stage 6 focuses on what is morally right as defined by self-chosen principles of conscience" (Loevinger, 1987:194–195, in Schriver, 2011, p. 169).

You will begin to develop an understanding of the relevance of spirituality during the life span cycle in your foundation course in HBSE; particularly as you review studies conducted with young adults who have experienced changes that influence their definition and perception of spirituality as well as their level of religious activity (O'Connor, Hoge, & Alexander, 2002; Stolzenberg, Blair-Loy, & Waite, 1995). Often referred to as spirituality, it is generally understood as a "person's or group's relationship with their highest or deepest values, and how those values are understood and the general human experience of developing a sense of meaning, purpose and morality" (Hudson, 2010; Schriver, 2011). In studying human behavior, you will come to understand the various milestones achieved during various developmental periods to include Freud's five stages of psychosexual development; Erikson's eight theories of psychosocial development; Piaget's four stages of cognitive development; and Kohlberg's moral development theory. Learning about and understanding these theories in your HBSE courses and the application of them in your field placement will better help you understand the biological, social, cultural, psychological, and spiritual development of your clients, and the end result will be better development of evidence-based service intervention and delivery. You will have the opportunity to explore these areas as well as practice them in your foundation year.

UNDERSTANDING OF KNOWLEDGE

Please choose the *best* answer from among the possible choices.

1. Lawrence Kohlberg's contributions include that:
    a. His theories cover the entire life cycle beginning with birth and ending with death.
    b. He was a physician and psychoanalyst who developed the psychoanalytic theory, which was the basis of psychodynamic theory used by social workers, and his theories have developed over time into ego psychology and object relations.
    c. His four stages of development focus on cognitive development through adolescence.
    d. His research was an outgrowth of Piaget's work and his focus was on the development of moral judgment.

2. The assumption that individuals, families, and communities all have the capacity for growth, change, and adaptation that must viewed through the lens of their capacities, talents, competencies, possibilities, visions, values, and hopes is best known as the:

   a. Systematic procedure
   b. Strength principle
   c. Strengths perspective
   d. Life course perspective

3. The life course theoretical foundation is across several professions and has been shaped by all of the following disciplines *except*:

   a. Sociologists and anthropologists
   b. Social historians and demographers
   c. Economists and mathematicians
   d. Psychologists and social workers

4. A group of persons who were born at the same historical time and who experience particular social changes within a given culture in the same sequence and at the same age is best known as:

   a. Cohort
   b. Followers
   c. Couples
   d. Families

5. Life events are a concept of the life course theoretical framework and are best known as:

   a. The long-term pattern of stability and change that usually involves multiple transitions
   b. The significant occurrences involving a relatively abrupt change that may produce serious and long-lasting effects
   c. The change in roles and statuses that represents a distinct departure from prior roles and status
   d. The events that produce a lasting shift in the life course

6. Clients belonging to groups and working within communities results in all of the following *except*:

   a. Helping to increase their sense of identity
   b. Creating a sense of isolation and seclusion
   c. Enhancing individual self-esteem
   d. Helping them obtain a source for social comparisons between themselves and others

7. The perspective that looks at how "chronological age, relationships, common life transitions and, social change shape people's lives from birth to death" is best known as:

    a. Strengths perspective
    c. Strength principle
    b. Systematic procedure
    d. Life course perspective

8. Sigmund Freud's contributions include that:

    a. His theories cover the entire life cycle beginning with birth and ending with old age.
    b. He was a physician and psychoanalyst who developed the psychoanalytic theory, which was the basis of psychodynamic theory used by social workers, and his theories have developed over time into ego psychology and object relations.
    c. His research was an outgrowth of Piaget's work and his focus was on the development of moral judgment.
    d. His four stages of development focus on cognitive development through adolescence.

9. From the life course theoretical foundation, you will be able to gain a level of understanding about the vibrant varying nature of person-environment transition and become familiar with all of the following *except*:

    a. The patterns in human behavior
    b. The concrete operations stage
    c. The diversity in the life course
    d. The unique life stories of individuals

10. This theorist proposed developmental stages that focus on critical developmental periods and the role of sexuality in development from infancy on:

    a. Jean Piaget
    c. Sigmund Freud
    b. Erik Erikson
    d. Lawrence Kohlberg

11. Erik Erikson's contributions include that:

    a. His theories cover the entire life cycle beginning with birth and ending with death.
    b. He was a physician and psychoanalyst who developed the psychoanalytic theory, which was the basis of psychodynamic theory used by social workers, and his theories have developed over time into ego psychology and object relations.
    c. His four stages of development focus on cognitive development through adolescence.
    d. His research was an outgrowth of Piaget's work and his focus was on the development of moral judgment.

12. Turning point is a concept of the life course theoretical framework and is best known as:

    a. The long-term pattern of stability and change that usually involves multiple transitions
    b. The significant occurrences involving a relatively abrupt change that may produce serious and long-lasting effects
    c. Those life events that produce a lasting shift in the life course
    d. The change in roles and statuses that represents a distinct departure from prior roles and statuses

13. Jean Piaget is well known for his contributions in:

    a. The development of moral judgment research
    b. The four stages of development focusing on cognitive development through adolescence
    c. The early social development theories
    d. The work on the systems theory

14. Kohlberg's moral development theory had three levels; the preconventional level, also known as the primitive level, is:

    a. Characterized by a member-of-society perspective.
    b. Where ethical reasoning is formed on the basis of general principles and is understood in accordance with underlying rules and norms.
    c. Where moral judgments are concrete and framed from an individual perspective that emphasizes following rules because rule-breaking may lead to punishment.
    d. Rooted in the ethical fairness principles from which moral laws are created.

15. Erikson explains his findings as:

    a. Socially and culturally determined
    b. The interpenetration of biological, cultural, and psychological factors
    c. Oedipal strivings
    d. Biologically determined forces

MASTERY AND ASSESSMENT OF
KNOWLEDGE OF SKILLS

Janice, a student social worker interning at local hospital, is discharging Domae Domino, a 56-year-old biracial male, after his two-day admission due to pneumonia. Mr. Domino explains that his daughter Gee and her son Desi brought him to the emergency room two days ago because of severe coughing and shortness of breath, and that he lives in Florida but was visiting them because Gee wants her son Desi to have the relationship with him that she could not, and she had invited him to visit. He explains to Janice that he had been a chain smoker for many years and attributed his shortness of breath to smoking and old age. Janice, the social worker, suggests to Domae that he will need a follow-up outpatient appointment with the clinic, but he indicates that he would be going back home to Florida, where he can be seen free at the clinic in his community. Domae also explains that he receives a small unemployment check and is anxious to get back to Florida and apply for some job so that he can keep his check going.

During the discharge planning with Mr. Domino and his daughter Gee, Domae begins to recognize how his adulterous relationships, the domestic violence, and ultimate divorce from Gee's mother impacted her as well as their relationship. Gee is also beginning to see the history of pain that her father experienced as a child in Nigeria and subsequently while living with his maternal grandmother after his mother abandoned him for a life of drugs. She learned that Domae's attachment to his grandmother was short-lived because of her mental illness and subsequent suicide when he was 14 years old, which put him in the foster care system until he was 18. The reality of his second abandonment later led Domae to a number of negative life events such as sexual addictions, drug abuse, and selling of drugs, which landed him in jail. Mr. Domino explains and Gee learns for the first time of her father's strong attachment for his mother and hatred toward his father around the age of four, directly before he left Nigeria. He talks about how he sometimes felt that he was in competition with his father for his mother's love.

Domae also talks about his loss of job, major health challenges, and a cocaine addiction. Gee also learns that her father had moved to the States with his mother when he was 11 years old, after the separation of his parents due to his father's adulterous relationships and spousal abuse. Although his grandmother's funeral was painful, Domae shares that he experienced a spiritual awakening at his mother's funeral that was a pivotal moment in his life that changed his mindset and ultimately altered his behavior. He stopped smoking cocaine, found a boarding room, and found stable and legal employment. Now that the economy is so bad, his employment opportunities have lessened; however, he for once is on the straight and narrow, avoiding breaking rules that are backed by punishment. A social worker working a situation such as Mr. Domino's must be aware that one discharge planning involves a life transition that is part of a larger life course.

Select the *best* answer using the Domino vignette.

1. Janice, the student social worker, is in her weekly meeting with her agency supervisor, Mr. Jackson, and he asks her about Mr. Domino's *event history* relative to her understanding of the life course perspective in analyzing human behavior. Janice's best response regarding identifying Mr. Domino's event history would be his:

    a. Being a chain smoker for many years, severe coughing and shortness of breath, emergency room visit, and living in Florida are the best examples of his event history.
    b. Getting a divorce, suffering his maternal grandmother's mental illness and subsequent suicide, sexual addictions during his adulthood, drug abuse, and selling of drugs, which landed him in jail, are the best examples of his event history.
    c. Relationship with grandson Desi, suggestion to seek outpatient treatment, and visiting his daughter are the best examples of his event history.
    d. His receiving a small unemployment check and being anxious to get back to Florida to apply for some jobs in order to keep his check going is the best example of his event history.

2. Damae's becoming addicted to cocaine and setting forth on a path of increased substance abuse, his failing abilities to maintain a relationship with his daughter Gee, as well as his multiple transitions involving family disruptions and employment instability, are all examples of the life course perspective concept best known as:

    a. Cohort
    b. Trajectory
    c. Turning point
    d. Life event

3. During a group discussion in her HBSE class, Janice shared that when Mr. Domino was four, he remembered having a strong attachment for his mother and hatred toward his father in which he sometimes felt that he was in competition with him for his mother's love. The theory that best addresses Mr. Domino's behavior is:

    a. Erik Erikson's psychosocial stages of development
    b. Sigmund Freud's psychosexual stages of development
    c. Jean Piaget's cognitive stages of development
    d. Lawrence Kohlberg's theory of moral development

4. Mr. Domino's strong attachment for his mother and hatred toward his father around the age of four is an example of the:

    a. Electra complex
    b. Preoperational stage
    c. Oedipus complex
    d. Initiative versus guilt stage

5. Domae's move to the States with his mother when he was 11 years old, after the separation of his parents due to his father's adulterous relationships and spousal abuse; the subsequent suicide of his maternal grandmother; and his four-year span in the foster care system are all examples of the life course perspective theoretical model best known as:

    a. Cohort
    b. Trajectory
    c. Turning point
    d. Transitions

6. The best response that would answer why Mr. Domino is more at risk to commit suicide would be because:

    a. Of his divorce from Gee's mother
    b. He suffers extreme financial loss
    c. Of a family history of suicide
    d. Of his visit with his daughter Gee and grandson Desi

7. Mr. Domino's experiences of loss through death by suicide of his maternal grandmother and the abandonment by his mother for a life of drugs were pivotal points in his life; however, the spiritual awakening he experienced at his mother's funeral that ultimately altered his behavior closely supports the:

    a. Psychosocial stages of development
    b. Theory of moral development
    c. Psychosexual stages of development.
    d. Cognitive stages of development

8. Gee, Domae's daughter, has requested to speak with Janice, the social work intern, regarding some concerns she is having about her family situation. Janice has decided to adopt the psychosocial approach to Gee's casework intervention. Janice would follow all of the following *except*:

    a. Meet Gee's needs of encouragement.
    b. Help Gee to deal with the problem of abandonment by her father.
    c. Endeavor to modify Gee's specific behaviors toward Mr. Domino.
    d. Lessen Gee's suffering and distress.

9. Janice has a session with Gee and learns that she was abandoned by her mother at 18 months, pregnant at age 17, and married at 24. She later has three additional children and at age 27 suddenly neglects her family, spending time going out socially with her female friends. Janice more than likely has problems with:

   a. Identity
   b. Object relations
   c. Trust
   d. Intimacy

10. In a session with Mr. Domino, Janice learned that while in his twenties, he had problems establishing satisfying sexual relationships with women, which subsequently led to a sexual addiction. According to Erikson, the phase of life crisis this situation represented was:

    a. Generativity versus stagnation
    b. Industry versus inferiority
    c. Initiative versus guilt
    d. Autonomy versus shame and doubt

Reflective Essay Questions

1. Discuss your views as to why knowledge in the traditional areas of personality and life span development are critical to social work education and evidenced-based practice preparation.

2. Discuss reasons as to why you believe different people react to the same type of stressful life events in different ways.

3. Discuss your views of the process of knowledge building regarding human behavior in the social environment that challenges first-year students and practitioners to explore the interplay between all aspects of human existence.

4. How would human behavior in the social environment change if it was first viewed from the perspective of social environment and human behavior?

5. What benefit can you achieve from your studies of human behavior in the social environment?

8

POLICY
PRACTICE

DETAILED UNDERSTANDING
AND EXPLANATION (DUE)

Policy is the driving force behind practice, and it can be an exhilarating process of learning because it entails the assessment of what humanity accepts as true concerning people. That is, the problems they experience, the typical process of resolving their issues, and what is fair and equitable when addressing them. During your foundation year, you will begin to understand the essential purpose of policy relative to your clients in your field placements. You will also begin to recognize the vital role you play when connecting policy with practice. In the foundation policy courses at your individual MSW programs, you will identify and become familiar with many important key concepts and perspectives of social policy and learn about diverse definitions of social welfare and their relationships to social work regarding the current structures of social policy and service delivery. As first-year social work students, you will continue to further your understanding as you begin to recognize social welfare, its value base and goals. In your overview of the history of social welfare policy, you will become skilled at applying critical-thinking perspectives to evaluate policies and programs that combat poverty. You will also come to recognize social policy as a process for policy formation and a product for policy implementation as you understand the characteristics of social welfare activities. This will aid you in better understanding the function of policy in service delivery and the role of practice in policy development.

There are many different definitions of policy, just as there are different interpretations of the programs that they drive and the organizations they maintain. Although social workers use policies in their practice, policy also has a place in all types of organizations, including governmental and national/international corporations and for-profit and nonprofit agencies, in addition to faith-based and academic institutions. A policy is a definite course or method of action selected from among alternatives and in light of given conditions to guide and determine present and future decisions; it is also the prescribed, governed, and practice activities or courses of actions adopted by formal organizations (Zastrow, 2010; Midgley & Livermore, 2009). Policies, essentially, are regulations that inform us which actions amid a huge number of actions we may perform and which ones we may not. Policies created and put into action by governments that deal with major issues, such as social, economic, political, and environmental matters, you will come to know as public policies. In your first-year policy classes, you will begin to learn that policies guide your work with clients and the decisions you empower them to make. You will be introduced to many terms, concepts, and ideas of policy practice, some of which you must promptly develop a clear understanding in order to progress your learning to the next level. A number of those concepts include, but are certainly not limited to, social policy, social welfare, social welfare policy, and the social welfare system.

Social policy is a decision made by public or governmental authorities regarding the assignment and allocation of resources, rights, and responsibilities, and expressed in laws and governmental regulations; or laws, rules, and procedures that regulate the reduction of social inequalities through redistribution of resources, rights, and social opportunities (Chambers & Wedel, 2009; Ambrosino, Heffernan, Shuttlesworth, & Ambrosino, 2008). You will learn during your foundation policy courses that social policy involves two facets: (1) the tangible guiding principles and programs of governments that affect people's welfare and (2) the academic field of inquiry concerned with the description, explanation, and evaluation of these policies (Midgley & Livermore, 2009). Some examples of social policies are the Social Security Act of 1935, the Personal Responsibility and Work Opportunity Reconciliation Act (1996), and the Patient Protection and Affordable Care Act of 2010 (PPACA). In your foundation policy class, you will acquire a working understanding of the social policies that you are most passionate about and most directly influence (1) your role, (2) your clients, and (3) the operation of your field placement agency. Some social policy areas or domains that will help shape your areas of policy interests are children and families and HIV/AIDS, community and neighborhood development, mental health and substance abuse issues, or immigration and refugee concerns.

Social welfare has many definitions that you will learn in your perspective MSW programs; however, you will come to view social welfare in both narrow and broad terms. In narrow terms, it is governmental provisions of economic assistance for persons in need that include those nonprofit functions of society, public or voluntary, whose aim is to alleviate distress and poverty (Dolgoff & Feldstein, 2009). The narrow definition of social welfare tends to include certain programs such as (1) TANF – Temporary Assistance to Needy Families, (2) Medicaid, (3) food stamps, and (4) child assistance. The broader definition of social welfare is a nation's system of programs, benefits, and services that help people meet needs that are fundamental to the maintenance of society, such as their social, economic, educational, and health needs. The broader definition tends to focus on formal rather than informal social institutions. You will come to learn in your foundation policy course that neither the narrow nor the broad definition is perfect.

Your understanding of the definition of social welfare policy will vary according to your professor and text; however, social welfare policy is a subcategory of social policies having to do with decision making regarding the problems of economic security and dependency (Dolgoff & Feldstein, 2009). Social welfare policies also are the laws and regulations that govern which social welfare programs exist, what categories of clients are served, and what qualifies for a given program (Kirst-Ashman, 2007). Fundamentally, you will identify with social welfare policies as being "anything a government chooses to do, or not to do, that affects the quality of life of its people and are influenced by the prevailing social values" (DiNitto, 2011). In your foundation policy class, you will come to understand that the social welfare system is the collection of programs, resources, and services available to help people in need, and these are the primary areas in which you will have internship opportunities within your perspective MSW programs. You will also find that the study of social policies causes you to examine your personal beliefs and values relative to those of your academic institution, your field placement, and that of your profession. As you comprehend the definition of social welfare, you will begin to understand its relationship to social work and the value base of social welfare.

You will quickly identify that the universal goals of social welfare are to fulfill the social, financial, health, and recreational requirements of all individuals in society (Zastrow, 2010; Jimenez, 2010; DuBois & Miley, 2011) and that the values of a society influence the nature of its social welfare system. Values are the assumptions, convictions, or beliefs about what is good and desirable or the way things should be (Ambrosino et al., 2008); they involve what you do and do not consider important and worthwhile and entail judgments and decisions about what is more valuable and what is less valuable (Kirst-Ashman, 2007). They also play a major role in the development and maintenance of our social welfare system, and those social and personal responsibilities are two key American social values that influence the creation of our public policies. Social responsibility is caring for the poor and those in need, while personal responsibility is self-reliance. You will come to understand self-reliance as the idea that each person is responsible for his or her position in society, which infuses public policy debates. If you agree that each person is responsible for his or her own circumstances, then public intervention is not valued.

In order to appreciate the present, it is sometimes important to understand the past. The review of the history of social policies that you will learn in your foundation policy course will be invaluable in your understanding of current structures of social policies and services. It is at this point in your studies that you will begin to understand that policy affects services delivery. You will learn that major influences in the development of the United States history of social policies date back to European approaches to social welfare as early as the Statute of Labourers of 1351 to the Elizabethan Poor Law of 1601 and the Speenhamland Act of 1795. The Statute of Labourers of 1351 was the first statute of poor law legislation that evolved over the next four centuries; while the Elizabethan Poor Law required that some able-bodied persons be made to work in poor houses and urged families to care for their own impoverished relatives. The Speenhamland Act was an amendment to the Elizabethan Poor Law, in which subsidies called the "bread scale" were used rather than regulating wages during times of short harvests from 1794 to 1795 (Dolgoff & Feldstein, 2009; Zastrow, 2010). You will also learn about historic landmark legislation such as the Social Security Act of 1935, the Personal Responsibility and Work Opportunity Reconciliation Act of 1996, and all the programs they created and services they provide. You will also begin to understand recent legislation in your foundation policy courses such as the health care reform bill that evolved into Patient Protection and Affordable Care Act of 2010 (PPACA) and the Health Care and Education Reconciliation Act.

You will learn that the Social Security Act of 1935, as one of the most prominent pieces of legislation of all time, established a structure of benefits in three major categories: (1) social insurance, (2) public assistance, and (3) health services. This legislation changed the course of the social welfare system and gave the federal government the responsibility to provide an organized system of resources for its citizenry. As a federal program operated by the Social Security Administration, social security covers 90% of the workforce and is the nation's largest social program (Day, 2009). You will come to understand the role of policy in service delivery in social work practice as you begin to identify with income maintenance programs administered by the Social Security Administration such as survivor's insurance/disability insurance, also known as Old Age, Survivors, Disability, and Health Insurance (OASDHI), and Supplemental Security Insurance. Survivor's insurance can be awarded to surviving minor children and their surviving parents and to dependent parents of deceased workers. Disability insurance is paid to disabled adults who are unable to work, while Supplemental Security Insurance (SSI) is a categorical means-tested public assistance program categorized for the poor such as the aged, blind, and disabled. Unemployment insurance, originally passed in 1935 as part of the Social Security Act, is where employers contribute to a state unemployment fund that benefits workers who are dismissed. Benefits are time limited and based on past earnings and length of employment.

The Personal Responsibility and Work Opportunity Reconciliation Act of 1996 (PRA), you will learn, eliminated the open-ended federal entitlement Aid to Families with Dependent Children (AFDC), which was a federal-state program that provided cash support to low-income families with children. In your foundation policy course, you will learn that PRA gave states the power to run their own welfare and work programs by creating state block grants to provide time-limited cash assistance for needy families called TANF, or Temporary Assistance for Needy Families (DuBois & Miley, 2011). You will further your understanding of the roles of policy in service delivery and practice in policy development after understanding recent legislations. The health care reform bill that evolved into the Patient Protection and Affordable Care Act of 2010 (PPACA) and was signed into law by President Obama on March 23, 2010, you will learn, will impact you and your future personally as well as professionally. The impact of this major health care reform bill and its promise to expand health care coverage to 31 million uninsured Americans will bring about interesting debate for your policy classes and hope for your client base at your internship. The Health Care and Education Reconciliation Act, along with the Patient Protection and Affordable Care Act, you will learn, promises to ensure that all Americans have access to quality, affordable health insurance, and puts students ahead of private banks (PPACA, 2010; HCERA, 2010).

As first-year social work students, you will improve your ability to analyze and formulate policies that advance the welfare of your clients as you learn the characteristics of social policies and the distinctiveness of the social welfare delivery system and understand the policy-making process. You will learn that most social programs' focus is on populations who are unable to meet their needs and require governmental intervention. In order to make appropriate program referrals and properly analyze governmental interventions, it is important for you to distinguish between residual and universal programs. Residual programs are also known as safety nets, and are means-tested programs that provide necessary assistance to those in need when the market or family is not equipped to do so. Means-tested is a "common criterion used to determine eligibility by evaluating all of the resources clients have at their disposal to determine means to pay for services or buy things for themselves" (Kirst-Ashman, 2007, p. 217). Universal programs are available to everyone regardless of income and are non-means-tested. TANF and SSI, and public education and unemployment insurance, are examples of residual and universal programs, respectively. You will learn in your policy class that the social welfare delivery systems include occupational, fiscal, and social services. Occupational assistance is social welfare benefits provided through the workplace, such as employee assistance, disability insurance, health insurance, and retirement benefits (Chapin, 2007). Fiscal benefits are social welfare benefits provided through tax breaks, such as deductions for dependents and medical deductions. Social services are services received free or on a sliding scale (ability to pay) through public or nonprofit private agencies (DuBois & Miley, 2011).

In your foundation policy courses in your perspective programs, you will begin to understand your professional responsibilities for the development and implementation of social welfare policies and programs created in response to social problems. You will learn how to engage in policy practice to advance social and economic well-being and to deliver effective social work services to your clients by understanding the nature of problems as well as different models for policy analysis. Your understanding the nature of social problems and the external influences that are fundamental to the creation and establishment of social welfare policies is but one step in this process of your learning. In your foundation policy courses, you will begin to understand the "traditional" ways of policy making as well as the strengths perspective model in policy development, with an emphasis on person-in-environment. The strengths perspective model focuses on removing external barriers to individuals in their attempt to fulfill basic needs such as food, shelter, education, clothing, etc. Moreover, the strengths perspective seeks to secure the input of individuals who are affected by these barriers and who can offer solutions to their problems.

You will improve your ability to advocate for policies that advance the well-being of your clients by learning the dimensions of the various approaches to the social policy-making process. Policy practice is "the efforts to change policies in legislative, agency, and community settings, whether by establishing new policies, improving existing ones, or defeating the policy initiatives of other people" (Jansson, 2008, p. 14).

In your foundation policy course, you will learn that approaches to consider when understanding the policy-making process generally include but are not limited to: (1) identifying the policy problem, (2) devising policy alternatives, (3) legitimating policy, and (4) implementing policy (Chapin, 2007; Popple & Leighninger, 2011). When identifying the problem, you can look from the lens of C. Wright Mills's private troubles and public issues, as you consider the conditions under which a problem affecting individuals translates into a social issue that merits public attention (Dolgoff & Feldstein, 2009). You will learn that the policy-making process that involves devising policy alternatives includes research and the synthesizing of data. The research process in this instance includes (1) locating the at-risk population and cataloguing any special characteristics, (2) reviewing previous policies, (3) identifying theories that explain the problem's causes and solutions, and (4) creating practice-based experiments to support alternative polices (Jimenez, 2010). Synthesizing data includes stimulating debate, discussion, and feedback in addition to revising mission, goals, objectives, and methods (Dobelstein, 1999). Legitimating policy is simply lobbying and enacting policy changes, while implementing policy includes carrying out orders that translate policies into actions and coordinating resources and expenditures. You will apply the knowledge you learned in your foundation policy class as you engage in policy practice through the internship opportunities at your placement agencies. As was mentioned earlier in this chapter, policy adherence is part of all agencies, organizations, and institutions, and your internships are no exception. Your expectations and that of your perspective programs and agencies influence policy development, such as the number of hours required before completion and the days in field, as well as the guidelines for evaluations.

UNDERSTANDING OF KNOWLEDGE

Please choose the *best* answer from among the possible choices.

1. The narrow definition of social welfare is best stated as:

    a. A nation's system of programs, benefits, and services that help people meet needs that are fundamental to the maintenance of society, such as their social, economic, educational, and health needs
    b. Governmental provisions of economic assistance for persons in need that include those nonprofit functions of society, public or voluntary, whose aim is to alleviate distress and poverty
    c. A federal and state program that seeks to ensure proper nutrition for mothers and infants
    d. Current efforts to place more responsibility on government and away from individuals/families

2. The assumptions, convictions, or beliefs about what is good and desirable or the way things should be, which involves what you do and do not consider important or worthwhile and entails judgments and decisions, is best known as:

    a. Policies
    b. The social welfare system
    c. Values
    d. Governmental considerations

3. Major influences in the development of the United States history of social policies date back to European approaches to social welfare as early as:

    a. The Statute of Labourers of 1351 and the Elizabethan Poor Law of 1601
    b. The Speenhamland Act of 1795 and the Personal Responsibility and Work Opportunity Reconciliation Act of 1996
    c. The Social Security Act of 1935 and Health Care Reform Bill
    d. The Patient Protection and Affordable Care Act of 2010 (PPACA) and the Health Care and Education Reconciliation Act

4. Originally passed in 1935 as part of the Social Security Act, the program where employers contribute to a state unemployment fund that benefits workers who are dismissed, in which benefits are time limited and based on past earnings and length of employment, is best known as:

    a. Disability insurance
    b. Supplemental Security Insurance
    c. Unemployment insurance
    d. Old Age, Survivors, Disability, and Health Insurance (OASDHI)

5. The legislation that eliminated the open-ended federal entitlement Aid to Families with Dependent Children (AFDC) and gave states the power to run their own welfare and work programs by creating state block grants to provide time-limited cash assistance for needy families, called TANF, or Temporary Assistance for Needy Families, is best known as:

   a. Patient Protection and Affordable Care Act of 2010
   b. Health Care and Education Reconciliation Act
   c. Personal Responsibility and Work Opportunity Reconciliation Act of 1996 (PRA)
   d. The Social Security Act of 1935

6. All of the following are accepted definitions of policy *except*:

   a. A definite course or method of action selected from among alternatives and in light of given conditions to guide and determine present and future decisions
   b. Major strategy for addressing poverty in the nonselective economic measures
   c. Regulations that inform us which actions amid a huge number of actions we may perform and which ones we may not
   d. The prescribed, governed, and practice activities or courses of action adopted by formal organizations

7. Programs that assist you in making appropriate referrals and aid you in analyzing interventions are called residual programs and are best defined as:

   a. Safety nets, and are means-tested programs that provide necessary assistance to those in need when the market or family is not equipped to do so
   b. Programs that are available to everyone regardless of income and are non-means-tested
   c. Social welfare benefits provided through the workplace such as employee assistance, disability insurance, health insurance, and retirement benefits
   d. Social welfare benefits provided through tax breaks such as deductions for dependents and medical deductions

8. Programs that tend to support the narrow definition of social welfare policy are:

   a. Food stamps and Medicare
   b. AFDC and social security retirement benefits
   c. TANF – Temporary Assistance to Needy Families and Medicaid
   d. SSI – Supplemental Security Insurance and educational grants

9. The landmark legislation that established a structure of benefits in social insurance, public assistance, and health services is best known as:

   a. Personal Responsibility and Work Opportunity Reconciliation Act of 1996
   b. Elizabethan Poor Law of 1601
   c. Social Security Act of 1935
   d. The Speenhamland Act of 1795

10. Examples of income maintenance programs administered by the Social Security Administration are:

    a. Survivor's insurance and disability insurance
    b. Housing and Supplemental Security Insurance
    c. Unemployment insurance and Women, Infants and Children (WIC)
    d. Old Age, Survivors, Disability, and Health Insurance (OASDHI) and food stamps

11. The policy-making process that involves devising policy alternatives via research includes all of the following *except*:

    a. Locating the at-risk population and cataloguing any special characteristics
    b. Reviewing previous policies
    c. Identifying theories that explain the problem's causes and solutions
    d. Eliminating practice-based experiments that support positive alternative polices

12. All of the following are definitions of social policies *except*:

    a. Decisions made by public or governmental authorities regarding the assignment and allocation of resources, rights, and responsibilities expressed in laws and governmental regulations
    b. Laws, rules, and procedures that regulate the reduction of social inequalities through redistribution of resources, rights, and social opportunities
    c. Decisions focused on formal rather than informal social institutions
    d. The tangible guiding principle and programs of governments that affect people's welfare

13. Some examples of social policies are:

    a. Children and families and HIV/AIDS
    b. Community and neighborhood development
    c. The Social Security Act of 1935 and the Personal Responsibility and Work Opportunity Reconciliation Act (1996)
    d. Mental health and substance abuse issues

14. The Patient Protection and Affordable Care Act of 2010 (PPACA) was signed into law by

    a. President Bill Clinton
    b. President George W. Bush
    c. President Barack Obama
    d. President Ronald Reagan

15. All of the following are accepted definitions of social welfare policy *except*:

    a. The collection of programs, resources, and services available to help people in need
    b. Anything a government chooses to do, or not to do, that affects the quality of life of its people and is influenced by the prevailing social values
    c. A subcategory of social policies having to do with decision making regarding the problems of economic security and dependency
    d. The laws and regulations that govern which social welfare programs exist, what categories of clients are served, and what qualifies for a given program

16. The universal goal of social welfare is to:

    a. To fulfill the social, financial, health, and recreational requirements of all individuals in society.
    b. To encourage the formation and maintenance of two-parent families.
    c. To provide employment for social work students upon graduation.
    d. To provide social welfare services only to individuals and families within a certain income range.

17. Examples of universal programs are:

    a. Public education and unemployment insurance
    b. TANF and AFDC
    c. PRA and SSA
    d. Food stamps and Medicaid

18. All of the following are approaches to generally consider when understanding the policy-making process *except*:

    a. Solving the cause of the problem
    b. Identifying the policy problem
    c. Devising policy alternatives
    d. Legitimating policy

19. The federal-state program that provided cash support to low-income families with children and which preceded Temporary Assistance for Needy Families is best known as:

   a. SSI – Supplemental Security Income
   b. AFDC – Aid to Families with Dependent Children
   c. Unemployment insurance
   d. Food stamps

20. The act of legitimating policy is to:

   a. Lobby and enact policy change.
   b. Coordinate resources and expenditures.
   c. Develop concepts and apply them to your clients' problems.
   d. Carry out orders that translate policies into actions.

MASTERY AND ASSESSMENT OF KNOWLEDGE OF SKILLS

Please choose the *best* answer from among the possible choices.

1. Sally is a student social work intern in her foundation year at I Can Help You Survive, a crisis intervention agency located in rural America. She is providing grief counseling to Julie, who has suffered the loss of her husband, Mitchell, two years ago due to an accident that occurred while working his federal job. Julie explains that she has exhausted all of their savings and has only one month of bill money saved up from Mitchell's life insurance, and that after that she and her two sons, Carl (age 10) and Richie (age 8) will have nothing. Sally should:

   a. Share with Julie that if she has not paid into social security then she must find a job and try to make ends meet.
   b. Share with Julie that survivor's insurance can possibly be awarded to her surviving minor children, Carl and Richie, if Mitchell paid into social security, and encourage her to go to her local Social Security office to apply for the benefits for her children as well as for herself.
   c. Share with Julie that she should go to the Social Security office, which is a governmental agency, and apply for Supplemental Security income because her husband Mitchell was a federal employee, and assure her that she will get it just based on his years served with the government.
   d. Say nothing regarding her financial woes but continue her grief counseling and explaining the grief process.

113

2. Julie is overjoyed with Sally's knowledge of the process of social security and tells her friend Monica to contact Sally. Monica, a 36-year-old female, explains that she is 100% disabled and has been told by several doctors that she can never work again because of her chronic arthritis. She explains that she has also been told by friends and family that she could never receive benefits from the Social Security Administration because she did not work a "real" job and was paid in cash or "under the table" most of her life. The best suggestion that Julie can make would be to:

   a. Refer Monica to her supervisor for further assistance.
   b. Say nothing regarding Monica's financial hardship and suggest that she look for another line of work to earn a living.
   c. Share with Monica that Supplemental Security Insurance (SSI) is a categorical means-tested public assistance program categorized for the poor such as the aged, blind, and disabled, and suggest to her to go to her local Social Security office to apply for SSI.
   d. Call her cousin who works at the Social Security office and tell her about Monica's situation, and ask her to look into it for her.

3. K. C. is a social work intern student in his first semester placement at Helping Hands, a temporary homeless shelter for men displaced due to economic conditions. Melvin, a 25-year-old resident of the shelter, has been looking for income streams since he lost his job and home. Melvin approaches K. C. with a question concerning a pamphlet that he received from the local welfare office. His question is regarding the definition of "means-tested." The best steps that K. C. should take would be to:

   a. Review the pamphlet and refer Melvin back to the welfare office where he received the information to safeguard against giving inaccurate information to Melvin.
   b. Explain to Melvin that "means-tested" is a common standard used to establish eligibility by looking at his resources to determine and prove his financial need.
   c. Suggest to Melvin that he speak with some of the other residents who might have gone to the welfare office and received the pamphlet.
   d. Say nothing to Melvin until he speaks with his agency supervisor or policy professor for guidance.

4. Peter, a very politically astute first-year student intern at the local Division of Family and Child Services office assigned to the Office of Family Independence, has noticed that the policies regarding the time limit of TANF have been unfairly administered to certain populations in a particular county. He speaks with his supervisor, Maria, and she disregards him and continues with her behavior. Peter wants to go directly to the governor's office; however, the best action for Peter to take is to:

   a. Discuss the pros and cons of possible decisions and actions with his mentor before he meets with his supervisor.
   b. Discuss the pros and cons of possible decisions and actions with his faculty field advisor who wiill speak with agency supervisor and/or agency director.
   c. Discuss the pros and cons of possible decisions and actions with his mentor before he meets with his supervisor.
   d. Discuss the pros and cons of possible decisions and actions with his mentor and the MSW field director and use role-play and simulations to rehearse the techniques, skills, or approaches he wants to utilize.
   e. Discuss with his policy professor how his decisions and actions fit with a particular conceptual framework, theory, model, or perspective.

5. Larry is a social worker at Positive Connections, a social agency that assists single fathers with children. Larry is seeking continuing cash assistance for Barry, who recently received a diagnosis of terminal cancer. Barry owns a $300,000 home in a middle-class community and owns two classic cars. The best place to refer Barry to would be the:

   a. Social Security Administration
   b. Unemployment office
   c. Department of Family and Children Services
   d. ABC Baptist Church

6. Rodney is providing social work assistance to a two-parent family receiving TANF. In his efforts to help the family, Rodney must remember that:

   a. The landlords are likely to try to evict families on welfare.
   b. The family and the social worker must develop strategies to move the family toward independence because of the policy regarding time limits for receiving benefits.
   c. He needs to refer the family to other welfare programs once the time limit cuts the TANF benefits off.
   d. The children will suffer emotionally and academically if the parents are unable to find income and have to leave their home.

7. The director of field education at an MSW program has placed students at "ICU" social agency. He learns that "ICU" has a history of denying promotions to people of color in which several lawsuits against the agency have been won by employees over the past few years, yet the agency has not taken any steps to correct the problem. The director of field education at the university should:

   a. Notify the agency of the school's concern.
   b. Notify the agency that student placement arrangements will be discontinued and place the students in another agency as quickly as possible.
   c. Not interfere in the agency's operations.
   d. Do nothing because the two students placed at the agency are not students of color.

8. Jon is a 35-year-old white supervisor of the investigation unit at KYE, a social service agency in a metropolitan city. Jon is attracted to Marissa, a 23-year-old African American MSW intern from the local HBCU (Historical Black College and University). Even though Marissa works at KYE, she works in the intake unit, which is a different division of the agency. Jon does not supervise Marissa and will probably never supervise her. The next best action for Jon is to:

   a. Go to his mother, who is the director of the agency, discuss his attraction to Marissa, and ask her what to do.
   b. Approach Marissa to see if there is a mutual attraction and if so encourage the relationship, but only after hours and outside the boundaries of work, and not confer with the policy guidelines or anyone in upper administration.
   c. Review the policy guidelines of the agency and proceed regarding its standards.
   d. Approach Marissa to see if there is a mutual attraction and if there is not, request that she be transferred to his department so that Marissa can become familiar with him professionally in hopes that a personal relationship develops, and not confer with the policy guidelines or anyone in upper administration.

9. Marissa, a 23-year-old African American MSW first-year student from the local HBCU (Historical Black College and University) is interning at KYE social services agency in a metropolitan city. She is excited about the opportunity to intern with such a prestigious agency and has high regard for the director and her family because of their outstanding contributions to the community. Marissa believes that Jon, one of the unit supervisors at the agency, is attracted to her, and hates the way she sometimes feels around him but refuses to believe that his actions are inappropriate and discounts it as Southern hospitality. The next best action for Marissa to take is to:

   a. Review the policy guidelines of the agency and the university policy and act accordingly.

    b. Approach Jon to see if he really likes her or if she is being paranoid.

    c. Go to her mentor or the director of field education, report her concerns and Jon's attraction to her, and follow their recommendations.

    d. Go to the director of the program in confidence, express her concerns and disappointments to her, and follow her recommendations.

10. Mona Road is a 21-year-old first-year MSW student interning at Boys to Men Reform Academy, a second chance home for troubled teens located in rural America. Ms. Road is very confident of her looks and prides herself in making people feel special. She is eager to learn the "ins and outs" of the agency and plans to take some steps to doing so. All of the following actions are appropriate and within the standards of the school policy, agency procedures, and professional standards *except*:

    a. Locate and read from cover to cover the agency manual and websites that describe agency policy, mission, history, and procedure.

    b. Request an early morning weekend meeting with the director to discuss the agency, and then schedule a late lunch meeting with the oldest resident to get his perspective, and then compare notes for a well-rounded perspective.

    c. Attend any staff meeting open to Mona and observe employee interaction.

    d. Request opportunities to be introduced to agency staff and write down their names and job titles to remember and learn their names and titles.

Reflective Essay Questions

1. Discuss how your personal and religious values and beliefs, the economy, and the current political environment affect your adherence to and evaluation of the social policies of which you are passionate.

2. Discuss several examples and outcomes regarding what happens when the pursuit of individual well-being is disrupted by occurrences not of our own doing.

3. Discuss how the Patient Protection and Affordable Care Act of 2010 has impacted you personally and professionally, and what population you have seen it help or envision that it will help the most in the future.

4. Discuss how the Health Care and Education Reconciliation Act has affected you personally and professionally, and what population you have seen it help or envision that it will help the most in the future.

5. Identify the two major programs that you see that the Social Security Administration provides, and discuss the populations that they serve as well as the client base that you will most likely work with and why.

DETAILED UNDERSTANDING
AND EXPLANATION (DUE)

Your practice class will primarily draw upon what you learn in your human behavior course. Additionally, your practice course will draw upon what you will learn in policy and research. Your practice courses will serve as guides for you when you discuss case studies and begin working with clients during your field experience. You become well informed about your clients as you learn how to do a psychosocial history, which will be your main method for collecting, integrating, and prioritizing historical information about your clients so that you are able to make an assessment and develop intervention strategies. The psychosocial history can help you in your work with individuals as well as with couples and families. Generally, it can include (1) identifying information about the child, couple, or family; (2) a statement of the presenting problem; (3) a history of the problem; (4) family background; (5) work history; (6) health issues; and (7) use of alcohol and or drugs. If you are working with a child, you would want to attain additional information to include developmental history such as delivery, infancy, early childhood, school history, ego strengths and weakness, and the child's current functioning.

There are many tools, such as the ecomap and genogram, that can be used in the assessment process, and which you will learn are handled in many different ways in field placement agencies. An ecomap is a tool that gives a picture of the family in its environmental setting, helps to identify and describe the significant community context in which the family exists, and demonstrates the flow of resources and energy into a family system (Boyle, Hull, Mather, Smith, & Farley, 2009; DuBois & Miley, 2011, p. 209). You will learn that ecomaps assist you and your clients in envisioning their environmental resources and constraints. The genogram is an important tool to use in your work with couples and families as well; it is a schematic diagram that illustrates the structure and interrelationships within a family in the form of a genetic tree. It can incorporate information from at least two to three generations such as names, ages, and dates of marriages, divorces, and deaths. Genograms can also contain descriptive information such as religious affiliations, occupations, ethnic or cultural issues, illnesses, or important life events if relevant (Boyle, Hull, Mather, Smith, & Farley, 2009; DuBois & Miley, 2011, p. 209).

In your practice course during your first year, you will recognize the dynamic context of practice as you begin to understand the purpose of social work and become familiar with the many different definitions of social work practice. The Council on Social Work Education (CSWE), which accredits undergraduate and graduate social work programs, explains that the purpose of the social work profession is to:

Promote human and community well-being. Guided by a person and environment construct, a global perspective, respect for human diversity, and knowledge based on scientific inquiry, social work's purpose is actualized through its quest for social and economic justice, the prevention of conditions that limit human rights, the elimination of poverty, and the enhancement of the quality of life for all persons (CSWE, 2008, p. 1).

While the National Association of Social Workers (2006b) defines social work practice as:

The professional application of social work values, principles, and techniques to one or more of the following ends: helping people obtain tangible services; counseling and psychotherapy with individuals, families, and groups; helping communities or groups provide or improve social and health services; and participating in legislative processes.

As you begin to identify with the purpose and various definitions of social work, you will better understand the active environment and perspective of social work practice.

In your first-year practice classes at your perspective MSW programs, you will also learn about generalist social work practice, person-in-environment, and the different levels of social work practice. Generalist social work practice can be defined as the use of the problem-solving process to intervene with systems of various sizes, including individuals, families, groups, organizations, and communities (Boyle et al., 2009). Generalist social work practice works directly with clients' systems at all levels or practice settings—i.e., micro, mezzo, and macro—and within a person-in-environment (PIE) framework. You will learn that micro practice is social work practice that involves working on a one-to-one basis with individuals, mezzo social work practice is working with families and other small groups, while macro practice involves working with organizations and communities or seeking changes in laws and social policies (Boyle et al., 2009). Person-in-environment (PIE) means that an emphasis is on the ecological model, which stresses that people continually interact with many systems (Miley, O'Melia, & DuBois, 2011), while the generalist view to social work practice provides an integrated and multileveled approach for meeting the purpose of social work; you will learn in your practice course that it has various definitions, which have a tendency to be distinguished by common sets of components of delivering social work services. As you become familiar with the many terms and concepts of social work practice, such as generalist social work and all of the ideas associated with it, you will also learn about the tenets of direct and multicultural practice in social work.

As a first-year student, you will learn that direct practice is the provision of services to individuals, groups, and families that includes therapy, counseling, education, and other roles designed to enhance the problem-solving capacities of clients, improve their well-being, and assist them in meeting basic needs (Boyle et al., 2009, p. 12). Direct practice also includes your being active in a number of roles, some of which were discussed in chapter 1 of this workbook, such as counselor/enabler, advocate, broker, case manager, facilitator. You will learn that because of the changing demographics and the shifting complexion of the work force as well as the diversification of America, it is increasingly important that you become a culturally competent social worker. In your practice course, you will learn about conceptual dimensions of multicultural social work practice. Sue (2006) defines multicultural social work practice as "both a helping role and a process that uses modalities and defines goals consistent with the life experiences and cultural values of clients." He explains in his definition that in multicultural social work, you must recognize client identities that include individual, group, and universal dimensions and that any form of helping that fails to recognize the totality of these dimensions works against important aspects of a person's identity (Sue, 2003). By gaining an understanding of direct and multicultural practice, you will begin to identify the practical steps needed in response to the emerging organizational, community, and societal circumstances of your clients at your field placements.

In your first-year practice course, you will learn how to discover and appraise the different environments in which your clients live by systematic and logical processes. You will be able to accomplish this by many methods, some of which are through your learning how to work with multicultural families and applying scientific approaches to evidence-based social work practice. Cheung and Leung (2008) speak of balancing the three perspectives of (1) time, (2) personal involvement, and (3) social justice when working with multicultural families. By the time perspective, they suggest that the "related past events of the practitioner's life be linked to some degree to his or her current practice and the client/worker relationship." From the perspective of personal involvement, they suggest that "the practitioner/social worker become well informed about how a client's culture might influence the practitioner's/social worker's own viewpoint on how problems will be defined and dealt with within the client's context." Lastly, you will learn that the social justice perspective suggests that you should "encourage positive outcomes that influence your client's life meaning, a family's self-sufficiency in managing problems, and a community's collaborative efforts to support equality of service provision and equilibrium of system interactions." In balancing these three perspectives, Cheung and Leung (2008) further suggest that you will be competent at "(1) integrating theories with past, present, and future orientations; (2) theories with experiential, existential, and equilibrium foci; and (3) theories promoting justice, equality, and respect."

In your first year at your perspective MSW programs, you will learn that many practice theories exist and that there is no "one-size-fits-all" for the creation of successful interventions for your clients. Therefore, it is important that you learn how to utilize scientific approaches that are evidence-based for your social work practice. O'Hare (2005) defines evidence-based practice in social work (EBPSW) as the "planned use of empirically supported assessment and intervention methods combined with the judicious use of monitoring and evaluation strategies for the purpose of improving the psychosocial well being of clients" (p. 6). He suggests that evidence-based practice is a procedural framework and not a new theoretical construct. You will learn that evidence-based practice "promotes the use of data to support continuation of the best practices and identifies ineffective or harmful practices so they may be changed or eliminated" (Sue, 2006). You will also learn valuable steps in conducting evidence-based practice in your foundation practice course. Bloom, Fischer, and Orme (2009) identify the five steps of evidence-based practice as: (1) develop a question, (2) find the evidence, (3) analyze the evidence, (4) combine the evidence with your understanding of the client and situation, (5) apply to practice and (6) monitor and evaluate results (pp. 16–19). You develop a beginning understanding of how to determine the most relevant services for your clients that support the emerging societal developments in many ways during your first year. Some approaches to that learning will best be demonstrated by your learning about strengths-based practices and their influence on social work practice. Ambrosino, Heffernan, Shuttlesworth, and Ambrosino . (2008) suggest that with the strengths-based approach to social work practice, focus is "on the strengths of the client system and the broader environment within which it functions rather than on the deficiencies." You will also come to understand the importance of the six basic principles of the strengths-based practice perspective and their application to your field placement experiences during your first year in your MSW programs. Saleebey (2009) cites the following six principles as the foundation of the strengths perspective:

1. "Every individual, group, family, and community have strengths";
2. "Trauma and abuse, illness and struggle may be injurious, but they may also be sources of challenge and opportunity";
3. "Assume that you do not know the upper limits of the capacity to grow and change and take individual, group, and community aspirations seriously";
4. "We best serve clients by collaborating with them";
5. "Every environment is full of resources"; and
6. "Caring, caretaking, and context" (pp. 15–18).

You will learn through this perspective that your professional role is to help clients resolve their own problems through their strengths and skills in efforts to reach their goals.

You will establish clear understanding of how to use knowledge and skill to respond proactively in your practice of social work during your first year by learning additional practice theories in your coursework and applying them in your field placements. There are many that you can draw from at your perspective school that have been empirically tested and shown to be effective that are briefly discussed in chapter 5 of this book, i.e., ego psychology, psychosocial theory, and psychoanalytic theory. However, you will also learn theories such as the person-in-environment (PIE), which you will find very beneficial for your practice in your field placement. The person-in-environment system evaluates problems in social functioning, i.e., social role performance, and focuses on balance and imbalance between persons and their environment. The PIE system uses four factors to describe client problems: (1) social-role problem, (2) environmental problem, (3) mental disorder, and (4) physical disorder or physical health problems (Ashford et al., 2006). Social-role problems are the social functions in which the type, severity, and duration of problems are identified along with the client's ability to cope with them; while environmental problems are the social system in which each problem is identified along with the types of problems within each social system, severity of problems, and duration. Mental disorder looks at the mental health of the client in terms of clinical condition plus developmental and personality disorder; while physical disorder looks at the physical health and diseases diagnosis of physicians and self-reported health problems by the client and others (Ambrosino, Heffernan, Shuttlesworth, and Ambrosino, 2008). You will learn that the person-in-environment perspective offers a more holistic approach and that you must consider all four factors necessary when describing clients' problems.

You will also learn to apply macro-level interventions in your field placements as you learn about practice with groups, neighborhoods, and communities. In your macro-level work, you will learn how to assist in resolving intergroup tensions. You will learn how to address determinants for social functioning for community problems by being a change agent for issues in the community such as housing, cultural diversity, and educational resources; societal issues such as prejudices, unjust laws, and unfair legislation; and world community issues such as human rights, hunger, and world poverty (DuBois & Miley, 2011). Summarily, your first year of foundation will focus on generalist practice and prepare you to move into your second year of advanced specialization/concentration. The second-year specializations or concentrations will allow you to focus your studies in an area in which you hope to practice. Specializations can include: Child and Family, Mental Health, School Social Work, Substance Abuse, Child Welfare, and Forensic Social Work, among others.

UNDERSTANDING OF KNOWLEDGE

Please choose the *best* answer from among the possible choices.

1. The definition for social work practice as defined by the NASW is:

   a. The profession that is actualized through its quest for social and economic justice that includes the prevention of conditions that limit human rights, the elimination of poverty, and the enhancement of the quality of life for all persons.

   b. The professional application of social work values, principles, and techniques to one or more of the following ends: helping people obtain tangible services; counseling and psychotherapy with individuals, families, and groups; and helping communities or groups provide or improve social and health services.

   c. A profession that promotes human and community well-being, guided by a person and environment construct, a global perspective, respect for human diversity, and knowledge based on scientific inquiry.

   d. The profession that seeks changes in laws and social policies by working only with organizations and communities.

2. The social work practice that is "both a helping role and a process that uses modality and defines goals consistent with the life experiences and cultural values of clients" is best known as:

   a. Mezzo social work practice
   b. Scientific social work practice
   c. Culturally sensitive social work practice
   d. Multicultural social work practice

3. The three perspectives that Cheung and Leung spoke of when working with multicultural families are best known as:

   a. Time, personal involvement, and social justice
   b. Time, economics, and personal involvement
   c. Personal involvement, social justice, and prejudice
   d. Human rights, social justice, and evidence-based perspective

4. The psychosocial history can help you in your work with individuals, couples, and families, and generally includes all of the following *except*:

   a. A history of the problem and family background
   b. Identifying information about the child, couple, or family and a statement of the presenting problem
   c. A picture of the family in their environmental setting
   d. Client's work history and health issues

5. The person-in-environment system, which evaluates problems in social functioning and focuses on balance and imbalance between persons and their environment, factors in the following:

   a. Social-role problem, environmental problem, mental disorder, and physical disorder or physical health problems
   b. Time, personal involvement, and social justice
   c. Human rights, social justice, and evidence-based perspective
   d. A picture of the family in their environmental setting

6. The *time perspective* that Cheung and Leung spoke of as one of the three perspectives to balance when working with multicultural families suggests that:

   a. "The practitioner/social worker become well informed about how a client's culture might influence the practitioner's/social worker's own viewpoint on how problems will be defined and dealt with within the client's context"
   b. The "related past events of the practitioner's life be linked to some degree to his or her current practice and the client/worker relationship"
   c. The practitioner/social worker should "encourage positive outcomes that influence the client's life meaning, a family's self-sufficiency in managing problems, and a community's collaborative efforts to support equality of service provision and equilibrium of system interactions"
   d. The practitioner/social worker should use multiple methods of data collection from multiple sources

7. Generalist social work practice is best defined as:

   a. The use of the problem-solving process to intervene with systems of various sizes, including individuals, families, groups, organizations, and communities
   b. The provision of services to individuals, groups, and families that includes therapy, counseling, education, and other roles designed to enhance the problem-solving capacities of clients, improving their well-being, and assisting them in meeting basic needs
   c. The practice that involves working on a one-to-one basis only with individuals
   d. The practice of only working with families and other small groups

8. The "focus on the strengths of the client system and the broader environment within which it functions rather than on the deficiencies" is best known as the:

   a. Person-in-environment system
   b. Strengths-based perspective
   c. Evidenced-based perspective
   d. Person-in-environment perspective

9. The main method for collecting, integrating, and prioritizing historical information about your clients is via:

   a. Ecomap
   b. Genogram
   c. Psychosocial history
   d. PIE

10. The environmental problem concept of the PIE system is best explained by:

    a. The social functions in which the type, severity, and duration of problems are identified along with the client's ability to cope with them
    b. The social system in which each problem is identified along with the types of problems within each social system, severity of problems, and duration
    c. Looking at the mental health of the client in terms of clinical condition plus developmental and personality disorder
    d. Looking at the physical health and diseases diagnosis of physicians and self-reported health problems by the client and others

11. An ecomap is best known as:

    a. A tool that incorporates information from at least two to three generations such as names, ages, and dates of marriages, divorces, and deaths
    b. A tool that gives a picture of the family in its environmental setting, helps to identify and describe the significant community context in which the family exists, and demonstrates the flow of resources and energy into a family system
    c. A schematic diagram that illustrates the structure and interrelationships within a family in the form of a genetic tree
    d. A schematic diagram that contains descriptive information such as religious affiliations, occupations, ethnic or cultural issues, illnesses, or important life events if relevant

12. The "planned use of empirically supported assessment and intervention methods combined with the judicious use of monitoring and evaluation strategies for the purpose of improving the psychosocial well being of clients" is best known as:

    a. Evidence-based practice in social work (EBPSW)
    b. Person-in-environment (PIE)
    c. Strengths-based practice approach
    d. Macro social work approach

13. All are basic principles of the strengths-based practice perspective *except*:

   a. Assessing clients' well-being on multidimensional levels and employing functional analysis

   b. Every individual, group, family, and community have strengths; trauma, abuse, illness, and struggle may be injurious, but they may also be sources of challenge and opportunity

   c. Assume that you do not know the upper limits of the capacity to grow and change and take individual, group, and community aspirations seriously

   d. We best serve clients by collaborating with them, and every environment is full of resources

14. The *social justice perspective* that Cheung and Leung spoke of as one of the three perspectives to balance when working with multicultural families suggests that:

   a. "The practitioner/social worker become well informed about how a client's culture might influence the practitioner's/social worker's own viewpoint on how problems will be defined and dealt with within the client's context"

   b. The "related past events of the practitioner's life be linked to some degree to his or her current practice and the client/worker relationship"

   c. The practitioner/social worker should "encourage positive outcomes that influence your client's life meaning, a family's self-sufficiency in managing problems, and a community's collaborative efforts to support equality of service provision and equilibrium of system interactions"

   d. The practitioner/social worker should use multiple methods of data collection from multiple sources

15. All of the following are examples of the steps for conducting evidence-based practice *except*:

   a. Going beyond general theoretical perspectives and using problem-specific knowledge

   b. Assessing clients' well-being on multidimensional levels and employing functional analysis

   c. Incorporating the client's unique understanding of the problem into the assessment and pragmatically emphasizing problems that are amenable to change

   d. Assuming that you do not know the upper limits of the capacity to grow and change and take individual, group, and community aspirations seriously

MASTERY AND ASSESSMENT OF KNOWLEDGE OF SKILLS

Please choose the *best* answer from among the possible choices.

Questions 1 to 4 are based on the following paragraph:

Virginia, a first-year MSW student, is interning at Moving Toward Maturity (MTM) an independent living center that provides a residential, vocational training program for older adolescents ages 17 to 21. Paul, an 18-year-old African American, and Robert, a 19-year-old Caucasian, are residents at MTM who were at one point both foster children to Ms. Patty. Paul and Robert learn that Ms. Patty has been accidentally killed by a foster child and seek counseling from Virginia. Virginia begins to counsel them and is genuinely concerned, but her supervisor, Ms. Smith, notices her "over-involvement."

1. The best action that Ms. Smith, Virginia's supervisor, should take is to:

    a. Arrange for an immediate transfer of social work services for Paul and Robert to a more experienced intern, possibly in his or her second year.
    b. Involve Virginia in assessing the effect her subjective reactions may have on the quality of her work with Paul and Robert.
    c. Commend Virginia for being so dedicated to her work, even as a student.
    d. Thoroughly explore Virginia's inner views regarding the nature of this tragedy and suggest the necessity for an immediate resolution.

2. Virginia should do all of the following *except*:

    a. Be open to Ms. Smith's observations and accept her feedback, then discuss them with her cohorts during her weekly seminar classes at her university.
    b. Be open to Ms. Smith's observations and accept her feedback, then discuss them with the director of field education at her university.
    c. Be open to Ms. Smith's observations and accept her feedback, then discuss them with Paul and Robert during their next session.
    d. Be open to Ms. Smith's observations and accept her feedback, then discuss them with her school mentor/advisor after her supervision with Ms. Smith.

3. Which of the following *should* be part of the treatment plan that Virginia creates for Paul and Robert?

    a. Triple the number of weekly sessions.
    b. Assure Paul and Robert that things will get better and that as time moves on, they will eventually forget about Ms. Patty.
    c. Arrange for an immediate transfer of social work services for Paul and Robert to a more experienced intern, possibly in his or her second year.
    d. Provide direct encouragement of positive outcomes that influence Paul and Robert's life meaning.

4. During a session with Virginia, Paul shares that the longest foster mother he ever had was Ms. Patty, from ages 8 to 13. He also complains that though he is usually energetic and optimistic, since Ms. Patty's death, he feels angry, unmotivated, and has noticed some destructive behaviors at MTM. Moreover, he has had trouble coping with important aspects of his life such as studying for his General Educational Development (GED) test, and is unable to settle down or complete his thoughts. In this situation, Ms. Patty's death is viewed as all of the following *except*:

   a. A statement of the presenting problem
   b. The precipitating stress
   c. A tragedy, with undue sympathy
   d. Relevant to his functioning

Questions 5 to 7 are based on the following paragraph:

Emanuel, a 35-year-old undocumented Hispanic male, comes to Larry, an intern social work student at the Community Services Board, for counseling because he feels inadequate due to his speaking broken English, not feeling as though he is providing for his family or their protector, and hopelessness about past personal decisions over the last month. Emanuel shares that he believes that he suffers from low self-esteem and needs help because he wants his family to respect him more and his community to feel better about his being a part of it. During the session, Larry helps Emanuel to change from an external blaming focus to an internal focus of taking charge of his life.

5. Larry's actions toward Emanuel are an example of:

   a. Confrontation
   b. Empowerment
   c. Advocating
   d. Educating

6. Larry also wants to help Emanuel by utilizing data that promote and support the continuation of best practice interventions. As an *evidence-based social work practitioner*, Larry's plan is to identify ineffective counseling techniques that he has used in the past with Emanuel and integrate a balance between theories with past, present, and future orientations. Larry can do all of the following to accomplish this, *except*:

   a. Go beyond general theoretical perspective when using problem-specific knowledge regarding Emanuel not feeling as though he is providing for his family or their protector.
   b. Evaluate Emanuel's well-being on multidimensional levels and design an intervention that examines his concerns of low self-esteem.
   c. Incorporate Emanuel's unique understanding of the problem of hopelessness regarding past personal decisions over the last month into the assessment.

d. Design an ecomap that gives a picture of Emanuel's future environmental setting that describes the significant community context in which the family exists.

7. Larry later learns that Emanuel's stated purpose is to receive help in adapting to his feelings of inadequacy and separation, rather than engage in a personal change process. Larry's approach to practice regarding Emanuel should focus on:

   a. Utilizing interpretation to help Emanuel to see the historical basis of his reactions
   b. Presenting concrete suggestions to manipulate the environment
   c. Helping Emanuel to respond to environmental and reality issues objectively
   d. Allowing Emanuel to talk in a free associative, nondirective manner to ease inner tensions

Questions 8 and 9 are based on the following paragraph:

C. J. is a social work student intern at a local psychological service center that accepts third-party payments. His supervisor, Jonathan, falls ill and is unable to cancel his appointment with Phillip, and asks C. J. to conduct the session. C. J. is familiar with Phillip's situation and feels confident that he can adequately conduct the session. Midway through the session, C. J. receives a text from Jonathan asking him not to forget to charge Phillip under his own name. C. J. is familiar with the process of billing and that it requires an MSW and/or a license.

8. The dilemma of C. J., the student social work intern, is that of:

   a. Confidentiality
   b. Ethical-legal considerations
   c. Moral considerations
   d. Depersonalization

9. The next step that C. J. must take regarding his supervisor's request is:

   a. Charge Phillip for the services rendered as his supervisor Jonathan requested.
   b. Follow agency policy and report his concerns to his school advisor immediately.
   c. Charge Phillip for the services rendered as his supervisor Jonathan requested and discuss it with his school advisor at the monthly seminar meeting.
   d. Terminate the session and not charge Phillip anything and say nothing to anyone.

10. Mr. Thomas and his 16-year old son, Avery, come to seek counseling at I Can Help counseling agency. Mr. Thomas complains that Avery is secretive, evasive, and refuses to share information about his activities and discuss any of his problems. Further evaluation reveals that this is an enmeshed family. As a therapeutic goal, direct social work practice would suggest all of the following *except*:

   a. Design interventions that enhance the problem-solving capacities for the challenges of communication between Mr. Thomas and his son, Avery.
   b. Design a practical intervention that seeks to improve their well-being.
   c. Design an intervention strategy that will allow flexibility regarding roles you play in the sessions, such as counselor/enabler, advocate, and facilitator.
   d. Design an intervention that supports individual treatment for Mr. Thomas, with Avery's autonomy as the focus.

11. Florence, a 29-year-old accountant, is convinced that her promotion was denied because two of the male account executives dislike her. She was told that due to her lack of experience they would not be able to promote her, but would consider her for promotion in eight months. Florence, who is aware that her friend Chrysta is in her first year in an MSW program, tells Chrysta that she knows they turned her down because she is too aggressive and that they will deny her promotion again. Chrysta's best response is:

   a. To say nothing to Florence, because you do not "social work" friends because of boundary issues.
   b. "Yes, you are probably too aggressive for them."
   c. "That is the way accounting firms are."
   d. "You may be right, but they offered to reconsider you."

Questions 12 and 13 are based on the following paragraph:

Sylvia, a 23-year-old psychiatric nursing student, and her two children, Joseph (age 6) and Kathy (age 5), live with her best friend Mitch one mile from her parents' home. Sylvia visits her parents every day and talks with them on the phone or texts them several times a day. Sylvia seems helpless and dependent and comes to see Harriet, a first-year social work intern, for counseling.

12. In designing an intervention for Sylvia, Harriet could focus on all the issues to address her concerns *except*:

   a. The signs received from her parents to continue to play a helpless and dependent role.
   b. Sylvia's poor self-image created in the past, which is being reenacted in the present.

c. The impact of her behavior on the family.

d. Her relationship with Mitch and the impression it gives because she lives with a person of the opposite sex.

13. To ascertain the best information regarding Sylvia, in the initial session, Harriet should first:

a. Ask Sylvia to write an autobiographical statement that includes her presenting problem, a history of the problem, family background, work history, health issues, and use of alcohol and/or drugs within the last twelve months.

b. Conduct a psychosocial history on Sylvia which will allow her to collect, integrate, and prioritize historical information about Sylvia's family so that she is able to make an assessment of her concerns and develop intervention strategies for her problems.

c. Encourage Sylvia to share her feelings with her family and process them utilizing some of the techniques learned during her training as a psychiatric nursing student.

d. Call Sylvia to conference her parents in at the next session and conduct a family session where she addresses the cues that Sylvia receives from them encouraging her to continue playing the helpless and dependent role.

Questions 14 and 15 are based on the following paragraph:

Willis is interning at the Helping Hands Homeless Shelter. It has become common practice at the shelter to have residents participate in the decision-making, running, and maintenance of the shelter. Jerome, a resident of the shelter, chooses not to participate in any of the administrative activities of the shelter but complains regarding any issues that he does not benefit from.

14. The best approach for Willis to take regarding Jerome is to:

a. Ignore him and mentally place him in the same category as the other nonparticipants.

b. Suggest to the director of the shelter that they make participation at some level a condition of remaining in the shelter.

c. Make him participate even if he does not want to.

d. Make participation mandatory.

15. Jerome remembers when he had no place go, no food to eat, and the number of shelters that turned him away. He realizes that he has not been acting fairly toward the Helping Hands Homeless Shelter and apologizes for his behavior and volunteers to participate. In a group session at the shelter, Willis notices that Jerome is dealing with guilt. The best approach Willis should take is:

   a. Always relieve Jerome's guilt.
   b. Help Jerome to see what he has done to feel the way he does.
   c. Accept and understand Jerome's guilt and allow him to vent.
   d. Help Jerome see that guilt is very unhealthy and find ways to rid him of it.

Reflective Essay Questions

1. Your interactions and activities at your field placement involve both professional and personal qualities. Identify and discuss ways in which you have negotiated a professional partnership with your clients and what contributes to the personal side of the relationship.

2. Discuss what it means to conduct the various levels of social work practice such as direct, micro, mezzo, and macro at your field placements and what talents, abilities, and knowledge you utilize to practice them.

3. Discuss how you have used evidence-based practice and the strengths-based approach to social work practice at your field placement, and how you plan to use them during your second-year placement.

4. Identify a dilemma and discuss how you will navigate through it utilizing Cheung and Leung's three perspectives of time, personal involvement, and social justice. Utilize examples from your process recordings from your field experience, past experiences as a social worker, and situations that you have heard or read about during your matriculation at your perspective BSW or MSW programs.

5. Discuss the person-in-environment (PIE) evaluation of problems in social functioning and cite examples that demonstrate your understanding of it.

10

ENGAGE, ASSESS, INTERVENE, EVALUATE

DETAILED UNDERSTANDING AND EXPLANATION (DUE)

In working with clients, you learn to engage them through the relationship and to develop an assessment and intervention strategies that will help them to achieve their goals. In this process, you will understand the value of empathy, genuineness, and acceptance while working with clients. Fischer (1973) defines empathy as "the helper's ability to perceive and communicate, accurately and with sensitivity, the feelings of the client and the meaning of those feelings" (in Miley, O'Melia, and DuBois, 2011) To create an environment of empathy means that you accurately sense the inner feelings and meanings your client is experiencing. This openly communicates to your client that you understand how it might feel to be the client and that you are able to "feel with" him or her. By demonstrating this behavior, you are able achieve a level of "controlled emotional involvement through your expression of empathy." That is, to "feel with" them conveys a response of understanding of their emotions (DuBois & Miley, 2011, p. 130). Your ability to express the objective caring and commitment to your client results in empathic understanding, which simply means to understand accurately the feelings, thoughts, and motives of another. Empathic understanding results in empathic communication, which reflects respect and nonjudgmental acceptance.

You will learn that genuineness and acceptance are also important characteristics when engaging the relationship of your clients to developing an assessment and intervention strategies. The condition of genuineness, also known as *realness*, *transparency*, or *congruency*, means that you are being completely open in the relationship and that you have nothing to hide and there are no professional fronts. Fischer (1978) believes that genuineness aids helping relationships and describes it as "a characteristic that facilitates communication and builds open relationships" (p. 199). You will look to create a comfortable environment in which your clients can "be themselves" when you demonstrate genuineness. Genuineness is not honesty in that being genuine does not equate to full disclosure of every thought and feeling relative to the client–social worker relationship. On the contrary, it means that what is shared is "a real aspect of themselves, not a response growing out of defensiveness or a merely 'professional' response that has been learned and repeated" (Fischer, 1978, p. 199). Acceptance means that you feel an unconditional positive regard for your client and refers to terms such as caring or prizing. You will learn that acceptance and respect are personal qualities that you must draw upon in building relationships with your clients.

In your development of intervention strategies, you will work with your clients to develop mutually agreed-upon goals and outcomes. You will learn to help clients resolve problems and how to negotiate, mediate, and advocate for your clients. You will have developed knowledge and skills to practice with individuals, families, groups, organizations, and communities. You will also learn how to evaluate your work with clients on many levels including single subject design. Your social work education will teach you to understand the profession's history, mission, values, and ethics. It will serve as a foundation in the development of your professional identity for certain roles such as counselor/enabler, advocate, broker, case manager, facilitator, organizer, educator, mediator, negotiator, initiator, coordinator, researcher, and public speaker.

Your understanding of the NASW Code of Ethics and its broad ethical base and values along with knowledge of self-determination, the informed consent process, professional boundaries, and confidentiality all shape your understanding for an ethical practice. Your understanding and ability to apply ethical principles to guide your professional practice will prove valuable to you in your second year and invaluable for your practice success after graduation.

Your knowledge of the tenets of critical thinking and its role in any profession, but particularly its importance in the social work profession, is vital not only for you professionally but personally as well. As discussed in chapter 3, critical thinking is essential in social work because it requires that you learn to question theories and assumptions about people's behaviors and actions, about policies and procedures, and about programs and interventions. You will witness the personal and professional benefits of your understanding Gambrill's (2006, p. 15) fifteen related skills and knowledge relative to the critical thinking process. With the changing demographical landscape of the social work population, your knowledge of and appreciation for diversity will be fundamental to your being able to work with people across a continuum of client populations. Your ability to engage diversity and differences in practice pivots on your qualifying diversity cognitively in your class work and literally in your practice during your foundation field placement. Subsequently, the importance of diversity must follow to your advanced and final year in your perspective MSW programs.

Your introduction to the principles of human rights and justice in your undergraduate liberal arts courses and rediscovery of advanced human rights and social and economic justice during your foundation MSW years are major understandings that you must master. Your conversational knowledge of the tenets of the Universal Declaration of Human Rights (UDHR) will promote your future efforts regarding social justice for your clients. Your understanding of NASW's renewed dedication to support and advocate for human rights concerns will encourage classroom discussions and fuel practice interventions in your field placements during your second year. Your understanding of terms such as social justice, oppression, discrimination, prejudice, racism, and economic deprivation will ensure that you help all clients to resolve their problems regardless of race, creed, sexual orientation, religious affiliation, etc. In doing this it will make certain that your efforts are toward a culturally sensitive practice for service delivery and intervention development for your clients.

Your understanding of the need to engage in research-informed practice and practice-informed research has a voice in current research texts, taught in research courses and discussed by your research professors during your foundation year at your perspective MSW programs. As discussed in chapter 6 of the workbook, the purpose of research in social work is to answer questions, acquire new knowledge, and learn better practice methods that will help clients. Practice evaluation and the utilization of research are important skills you will begin to learn during your foundation year and perfect during your advanced year. Your understanding of the association between human diversity and the research process will help to facilitate changes for endings and conclusions and make possible changes for intervention. You will also begin to learn the relevance of your field practice experience and the implications its interpretation has on the development of your research skills, which will assist you in the assessment process for collecting, organizing, and interpreting client data.

Research skills such as conceptualizing a problem, formulating hypotheses and objectives, and designing research strategy will aid you in the assessment of the strengths and limitations of your clients. Your understanding of commonly used terminologies and research designs such as theory, hypothesis, independent variable, dependent variable, operationalizing, and conceptualization will increase your practice knowledge and use of research and technological advances. Your ability to critically analyze, monitor, and evaluate interventions for your clients is verified by your beginning to understand the inherent problems in some research designs and their implementation. It is then that you will begin to secure a basic understanding of the use of descriptive research, correlational studies, cross-sectional studies, and developmental studies in interpreting and evaluating research. Your beginning understanding of theory will help identify what will be needed before developing or organizing an intervention program for your clients. Understanding of this process will provide insight into how to shape program strategies that reach organizational goals and positively impact clients, and confirms your practice knowledge regarding the ability to evaluate program outcomes and practice effectiveness.

Your understanding of the strengths perspective, your knowledge of human behavior across the life cycle, the life course theoretical foundation and basic concepts such as cohort, transition, trajectory, life event, and turning point will help in your application of knowledge regarding human behavior and the social environment. Your understanding of key theorists such as Sigmund Freud, Erik Erikson, Jean Piaget, and Lawrence Kohlberg will help you apply theory and utilize conceptual frameworks to guide the process of assessment, intervention, and evaluation in human behavior. Your ability to identify and become familiar with many important key concepts and perspectives of social policy will increase your knowledge, values, and skills regarding the effects policies have on service delivery. As you learn about diverse definitions of social welfare and their relationships to social work regarding the current structures of social policy and service delivery, you will learn how to analyze and formulate policies for your clients. As discussed in chapter 8, you will improve your ability to analyze and formulate policies that advance the welfare of your clients as you learn the characteristics of social policies and distinctiveness of the social welfare delivery system and understand the policy-making process.

You will learn that most social programs' focus is on populations who are unable to meet their needs and require governmental intervention. You will learn how to provide leadership for policy formation and service delivery as you review the canons of historic legislation, from the Social Security Act of 1935 to the Personal Responsibility and Work Opportunity Reconciliation Act of 1996. You will learn how to create the best programs and interventions for your clients as you lobby for and advocate with your clients regarding new legislations such as the Patient Protection and Affordable Care Act of 2010 and the Health Care and Education Reconciliation Act. All of which will result in your engaging in policy practice that advances social and economic well-being for the impoverished, the downtrodden, and the "have-nots" in the delivery of effective social work service.

During your foundation year, you will be able to respond to contexts that shape practice by learning about clients through the use of social work practice tools such as the psychosocial history, genograms, and ecomaps. You will be able to identify, analyze, and implement evidence-based interventions designed to achieve client goals after your beginning understanding of Thomas O'Hare's seven steps to conducting evidenced-based practice in social work. You will substantively and effectively prepare for action with individuals, families, groups, organizations, and communities after gaining an understanding of generalist social work practice, person-in-environment, and the different levels of social work practice. By learning about the six principles of strengths-based practices and their influence on social work practice, you will discover how to select appropriate intervention strategies and develop mutually established and agreed-on interventions that support client goals and program objectives. As you learn how to address determinants for social functioning for community problems, you will begin to learn how to initiate actions to achieve organizational goals and implement prevention interventions that enhance client capacities. Conversely, learning how to navigate across all dimensions of social work practice, such as multicultural social work practice and evidence-based practice in social work (EBPSW), will help you to implement prevention interventions that enhance client capacities and initiate actions to achieve organizational goals.

After the completion of your foundation year in your perspective MSW programs, you will have gained the necessary knowledge, values, and skills to successfully engage, assess, intervene with, and evaluate individuals, families, groups, organizations, and communities. At this point in your foundation year, you would have learned to use empathy and other interpersonal skills, such as genuineness and acceptance. Your success in your foundation courses such as human behavior in social environment, research, practice, and policy will be products of your hard work and the application of understanding regarding the Educational Policy and Accreditation Standards. Your professional social work education will prepare you with the knowledge, skills, and values you will use to function effectively as a beginning social worker. You are now prepared to move into your second year of advanced social work practice.

UNDERSTANDING OF KNOWLEDGE

Please choose the *best* answer from among the possible choices.

1. The condition of being completely open in the relationship with your client and maintaining that you have nothing to hide and there are no professional fronts is best known as:

    a. Acceptance
    b. Empathic understanding
    c. Critical thinking
    d. Genuineness

2. The social worker in the role of a researcher does all of the following *except*:

    a. Select interventions such that he or she can monitor the progress of clients and evaluate their effectiveness.
    b. Have knowledge of the evidence-based process to ensure that programs, services, and interventions are appropriately matched with client needs.
    c. Bring together persons who are in conflict so that a bargain or compromise can be agreed upon and implemented.
    d. Analyze literature on particular clinical topics so that his or her practice will be current and "cutting edge."

3.	To create an environment in which you accurately sense the inner feelings and meanings your client is experiencing and openly communicate to your client that you understand how it might feel to be the client and that you are able to "feel with" them is best described by:

	a.	Acceptance
	b.	Empathy
	c.	Genuineness
	d.	Sympathy

4.	Feeling an unconditional positive regard for your client, and sometimes referred to by terms such as caring or prizing, is best known as:

	a.	Acceptance
	b.	Empathy
	c.	Genuineness
	d.	Sympathy

5.	Achieving a level of "controlled emotional involvement" with your client is best expressed through:

	a.	Realness
	b.	Congruency
	c.	Empathy
	d.	Genuineness

6.	The governing body that forms the foundation of the profession's values, defines the principles and standards for everyday behaviors for all social workers, and defines the ethical responsibilities for social workers is best known as the:

	a.	CSWE Doctrine of Fairness and Respect
	b.	GRE Standards of Acceptance
	c.	CSWE Code of Conduct
	d.	NASW Code of Ethics

7.	Relative to policy, AFDC is:

	a.	Financed totally by the state.
	b.	A program for families with children that was abolished in 1996 as a result of the Personal Responsibility Work and Reconciliation Act and replaced by a block grant popularly known as Temporary Assistance for Needy Families (TANF).
	c.	Financed totally by private citizens.
	d.	The only federal grant program under the Social Security Act.

8. Critical thinking in social work is essential because of the following:

   a. It requires that you learn to question theories and assumptions about people's behaviors and actions.
   b. It is a requirement of the curriculum.
   c. It is a good mental exercise for problem solving for your clients when they are in a crisis.
   d. It is great for assignments and presentations for social work students.

9. All of the following are appropriate and acceptable in an effort to ensure that you help *all* clients to resolve their problems regardless of race, creed, sexual orientation, or religious affiliation, *except*:

   a. Understand the NASW's renewed dedication to support and advocate for human rights concerns.
   b. Understand terms such as social justice, oppression, discrimination, and prejudice and their impact on your client population.
   c. Have conversational knowledge of the tenets of the Universal Declaration of Human Rights (UDHR).
   d. Subscribe to the philosophy that you must stay within your own race, gender, sexual orientation, and religious affiliation when providing services to those who are in dire need.

10. The best response that describes the purpose of research in social work practice is:

   a. To advocate and to confront oppression.
   b. To answer questions, acquire new knowledge, and learn better practice methods that will help clients.
   c. To stereotype and generalize about people because of their problems.
   d. To contribute to the general theories of treatment and cause and effect.

11. Your understanding of theory can do all of the following *except*:

   a. Help pinpoint what is needed before developing or organizing an intervention program.
   b. Provide insight into how to shape program strategies to reach youth and organizations.
   c. Eliminate societal issues such as prejudices, unjust laws, and unfair legislations and world community issues such as human rights, hunger, and world poverty.
   d. Help identify what should be monitored, measured, and/or compared with regard to other interventions.

12. All of the following are key human behavior theorists *except*:

   a. Sigmund Freud
   b. Jane Addams
   c. Erik Erikson
   d. Jean Piaget

13. All of the following legislations are as recent as fifteen years *except*:

   a. Social Security Act
   b. Personal Responsibility and Work Opportunity Reconciliation Act
   c. Patient Protection and Affordable Care Act
   d. Health Care and Education Reconciliation Act

14. The acronym EBPSW stands for:

   a. Evidence-borrowed practice in social work
   b. Evidence-biased practice in social work
   c. Evidence-based practice in social work
   d. Evidence-believed practice in social work

15. All of the following are social work practice tools, *except*:

   a. Psychosocial history
   b. Genograms
   c. Ecomaps
   d. Autobiographical statement

MASTERY AND ASSESSMENT OF KNOWLEDGE OF SKILLS

Please choose the *best* answer from among the possible choices.

1. Jessie is a social work intern at Families Now counseling agency. She is conducting a family session with Andrew (age 14) and James Jr. (age 17) and their parents Kathy and James regarding marital issues. Kathy and James dominate the session by putting the blame of their marital conflicts on their children. Jessie should:

   a. Open the floor to others in the session.
   b. Ignore Kathy and James.
   c. Ask Kathy and James to allow Andrew and James Jr. to speak.
   d. Ask Kathy and James to leave.

2. One of your clients requires an immediate therapeutic intervention that you have no training for and just do not know much about the method. You should:

   a. Get a co-therapist to work with you and the client.
   b. Conduct an intense literature review of the treatment method and try to give the treatment.
   c. Utilize a treatment method with which you are familiar.
   d. Refer the client to another therapist who is familiar with the treatment method.

3. Mr. Peters., who recently separated from his wife, and his two daughters ages fourteen and nine, are in a session with Joanne, a student intern at Yes We Can Counseling Center. Mr. Peters' initial complaint is that his nine-year-old daughter refuses to go to school, and that every method that he has tried to get her to go to school has failed. The first intervention by Joanne should be to:

   a. Arrange a home school system for his nine-year-old daughter.
   b. Inquire about whether Mr. Peters. wants help with the marriage.
   c. Help Mr. Peters take charge by insisting that his nine-year-old daughter go to school.
   d. See his nine-year-old daughter and Mr. Peters separately to explore their feelings.

4. Wendy, a 13-year-old Hispanic female, has stopped attending school and stays home. Harrell, a first-year school social work intern, has ruled out school phobia, trauma, bullying, etc., as reasons. The next action Harrell should take is to:

   a. Arrange for a tutor and begin treatment at home.
   b. Refer Wendy to a psychiatrist for medication and arrange for a rapid return to his school.
   c. Let Wendy stay home while offering treatment.
   d. Encourage Wendy's parents and the school to urge Wendy to go back to school as quickly as possible, and explore the reasons for her resistance.

5. Emmanuel, a 42-year-old Hispanic male, and his 13-year-old daughter Wendy are in your office for a session because of allegations that Emmanuel inappropriately touched one of Wendy's friends. Emmanuel speaks broken English and requires an interpreter. The least appropriate person to interpret is most likely:

   a. A relative
   b. An agency staff member such as a clerk or maintenance worker
   c. His daughter Wendy
   d. An untrained interpreter

6. A social worker is consistently late, fails to complete work on time, and completes forms carelessly. Though aware of the situation for some time, the supervisor does not confront the issue. Finally, the supervisor raises the worker's performance issues at a supervisory conference. The supervisee feels relieved and begins to discuss personal and family problems that have interfered with work. To move the discussion along relevant lines, the supervisor might interject:

    a. "I understand how difficult getting back to the issues I raised is, but…"
    b. "I know how difficult it must be. I had similar difficulties."
    c. "Have you considered a leave of absence?"
    d. "I understand how hard it is to function under such difficult circumstances."

7. Joanne, a student social worker, is considering terminating her client, Bobby. Joanne should focus on all of the following factors, *except*:

    a. Bobby's sense of loss
    b. Establishing outcome objectives for Bobby
    c. Her feelings about the termination
    d. Evaluating accomplished goals with Bobby before the termination

8. B. J., a Haitian adolescent male, is in conflict with his family and culture over his American ways. He wants to date, have friends, dress like others, and go to parties, and he feels very guilty. One of the things he needs that would help him most would be:

    a. That his parents take a class in acculturation
    b. That he and his family begin family counseling
    c. A social worker who specializes in Haitian issues
    d. The support of his peers

9. Dexter is a social work intern working at a suicide hotline. A person calls the hotline and says that he is going to kill himself. Dexter should:

    a. Find out his location.
    b. Establish rapport.
    c. Assess the situation in an attempt to clarify how serious he is.
    d. Ask him if he is alone.

10. Michael, a 15-year-old male, complains that his father has been inappropriately touching him. Kenneth, the social work intern conducting the home assessment, should talk first with:

    a. The father alone
    b. All of the members of the household

    c. Both parents at the same time

    d. The father, and then alone with Michael

11. A six-year-old male comes to school with bruises. The school social worker has the child in his office, but only a police officer is authorized to take the child for medical care. The officer refuses. The school social worker should:

    a. Ask the school administrators to become involved.

    b. Take the child himself.

    c. Call the officer's supervisor.

    d. Call his own supervisor.

12. You are the supervisor of an alcoholic employee. Your first responsibility is to:

    a. Refer him to the Employee Assistant Program counselor.

    b. Explore if the drinking has affected his job performance.

    c. Confront the person with his drinking.

    d. Suspend the employee until he stops drinking.

13. A male social worker realizes in supervision that he is attracted to a male client. The supervisor should *first*:

    a. Tell him to transfer the client immediately.

    b. Ask him to describe his feelings about the client.

    c. Ask if he's felt the same way about other male clients.

    d. Confront him with the inappropriateness of his feelings.

14. In working with a divorcing couple, the social worker tries to:

    a. Make viable plans for their children.

    b. Help them divide the property equally.

    c. Mediate until the couple is better able to deal with each other.

    d. Assess strengths and weaknesses in the couple's negotiations.

15. A family recently arrived from China and speaks very little English. They have just moved to the school district. As the school social worker, you should first:

    a. Obtain past school records.

    b. Obtain an interpreter with the consent of the family.

    c. Mainstream the child.

    d. Place the child in special education.

Reflective Essay Questions

1. Identify and discuss a social ill and a population that you are passionate about, and what drives your motivation to help them. Then identify a policy and a therapeutic model that that you would endorse and fund if you had unlimited resources to ameliorate that social ill.

2. Discuss the importance of your understanding of the correlation between policy and practice, and identify two challenges you fear regarding the Patient Protection and Affordable Care Act of 2010.

3. Discuss how problems and concerns addressed during your class, by your agency, and in personal conversation relate to other broad social problems such as poverty, crime, racism, high rates of divorce, the foreclosure epidemic, and the lack of affordable housing.

4. Discuss agency policies, procedures, and behavioral norms that you have noticed that tend to undermine and discourage social work professionalism within your colleges/universities, your agencies, and your county.

5. Discuss organizations you should join as a professional social worker in order to continue to enhance your professional development and knowledge base.

APPENDIX A

ANALYZING YOUR KNOWLEDGE AND SKILLS

CHAPTER 1

Understanding of Knowledge

1. c	6. c	11. b	16. b
2. b	7. b	12. a	17. d
3. b	8. a	13. c	18. b
4. a	9. b	14. b	19. d
5. d	10. a	15. a	

CHAPTER 2

Understanding of Knowledge

1. d	5. d	9. b	13. c
2. a	6. d	10. c	14. d
3. b	7. d	11. b	15. b
4. c	8. a	12. c	

CHAPTER 3

Understanding of Knowledge

1. d	5. c	9. a	13. b
2. b	6. c	10. c	14. c
3. c	7. d	11. b	15. d
4. a	8. a	12. a	

CHAPTER 4

Understanding of Knowledge

1.	b	5.	c	9.	c	13.	c
2.	a	6.	a	10.	a	14.	b
3.	c	7.	b	11.	d	15.	d
4.	d	8.	d	12.	d		

CHAPTER 5

Understanding of Knowledge

1.	c	5.	c	9.	a	13.	b
2.	c	6.	b	10.	c	14.	c
3.	c	7.	c	11.	b	15.	b
4.	c	8.	b	12.	a		

CHAPTER 6

Understanding of Knowledge

1.	c	5.	c	9.	c	13.	b
2.	b	6.	b	10.	d	14.	a
3.	c	7.	b	11.	b	15.	b
4.	a	8.	c	12.	a		

CHAPTER 7

Understanding of Knowledge

1.	d	5.	b	9.	b	13.	b
2.	c	6.	b	10.	c	14.	c
3.	c	7.	d	11.	a	15.	b
4.	a	8.	b	12.	c		

CHAPTER 8

Understanding of Knowledge

1.	b	6.	b	11.	d	16.	a
2.	c	7.	a	12.	c	17.	a
3.	a	8.	c	13.	c	18.	a
4.	c	9.	c	14.	c	19.	b
5.	c	10.	a	15.	a	20.	a

CHAPTER 9

Understanding of Knowledge

1.	b	5.	a	9.	c	13.	a
2.	d	6.	b	10.	b	14.	c
3.	a	7.	a	11.	b	15.	d
4.	c	8.	b	12.	a		

CHAPTER 10

Understanding of Knowledge

1.	d	5.	c	9.	d	13.	a
2.	c	6.	d	10.	b	14.	c
3.	b	7.	b	11.	c	15.	d
4.	a	8.	a	12.	b		

Addis, M.E., and A.D. Krasnow. 2000. A national survey of practicing psychologists'attitudes toward psychotherapy treatment manuals. *Journal of Consulting and Clinical Psychology* 68:331–339.

Albert, R. 1983. Social advocacy in the regulatory process. *Social Casework* 64:473–481.

Alwin, D., and R. McCammon. 2003. Generations, cohorts, and social change. In *Handbook of the life course*, ed. J. Mortimer and M. Shanahan, 23–49. New York: Kluwer Academic/Plenum Publishers.

Ambrosino, R., J. Heffernan, G. Shuttlesworth, and R. Ambrosino. 2008. *Social work and social welfare: An introduction.* 6th ed. Belmont, Calif: Brooks/Cole.

American Psychiatric Association. 2000. *Diagnostic and statistical manual of mental disorders*. 4th ed. rev. Washington, D.C.: American Psychiatric Association.

Ashford, J., C. LeCroy, and K. Lortie. 2006. *Human behavior in the social environment: A multidimensional perspective*. 3rd ed. Pacific Grove, Calif.: Brooks/Cole.

Austin, D.M. 1983. The Flexner myth and the history of social work. *Social Service Review* 57:357–376.

Baer, D.M. 2003. Program evaluation: Arduous, impossible, or political? In *Using evidence in social work practice: Behavioral perspectives*, ed. H.E. Briggs and T.L. Rzepnicki. Chicago: Lyceum.

Barker, R.L. 2003. *The social work dictionary*. 5th ed. Washington, D.C.: NASW Press.

Barlett, H.M. 1970. *The common base of social work practice*. New York: National Association of Social Workers.

Baron, J. 2000. *Thinking and deciding*. 3rd ed. New York: Cambridge University Press.

Baron, J. 2005. Normative models of judgment and decision making. In *Blackwell handbook of judgment and decision making*, ed. D.J. Koehler and N. Harvey. Malden, Mass.: Blackwell.

Baron, J.B. and R.J. Sternberg. 1993. *Teaching thinking skills: Theory and practice.* New York: Freeman.

Bell, L.A. 1997. Theoretical foundations for social justice education. In *Teaching for diversity and social justice*: A sourcebook, ed. M. Adams, L.A. Bell, and P. Griffin. New York: Routledge.

Bell, P., and M.C. Linn. 2002. Beliefs about science: How does science instruction contribute? In *Personal epistemology: The psychology of beliefs about knowledge and knowing*, ed. B.K. Hofer and P.R. Pintrich, 321–345. Mahwah, N.J.: Erlbaum.

Berg, B. 2009. *Qualitative research methods for the social sciences*. Boston: Allyn & Bacon.

Billingsley, A. 1968. *Black families in White America*. Englewood Cliffs, N.J.: Prentice Hall.

Billingsley, A., ed. 1994. The Black church. *National Journal of Sociology* 8:1–2.

Bloom, M., J. Fischer, and J.G. Orme. 2009. *Evaluating practice: Guidelines for the accountable professional*. Boston: Allyn & Bacon.

Boyd-Franklin, N. 2003. *Black families in therapy: A multisystems approach*. New York: Guilford Press.

Boyle, S.W., G.H. Hull, J.H. Mather, L.L. Smith, and O.W. Farley. 2009. *Direct practice in social work*. 2nd ed. Boston: Pearson/Allyn & Bacon.

Brandeis, L.D., and S.D. Warren. 1890. The right to privacy. *Harvard Law Review* IV(5) December 15.

Brittan, A., and M. Maynard. 1984. *Sexism, racism and oppression*. New York: Basil Blackwell Publisher.

Brookfield, S. 1995. *Becoming a critically reflective teacher*. San Francisco: Jossey-Bass.

Busfield, J. 2001. *Rethinking the sociology of mental health*. Malden, Mass.: Blackwell.

Center for Economic and Social Justice. 2010. *Defining economic and social justice*. Retrieved June 15, 2010, from http://www.cesj.org/thirdway/economicjustice-defined.htm.

Chambers, D.E., and K.R. Wedel. 2009. *Social policy and social programs: A method for the practical public policy analyst*. 5th ed. Boston: Allyn & Bacon.

Chapin, R. 2007. *Social policy for effective practice: A strengths approach*. New York: McGraw-Hill.

Chestang, L. 1972. Character development in a hostile society (Occasional Paper No. 3). School of Social Service Administration. Chicago: University of Chicago Press.

Cheung, M., and P. Leung. 2008. *Multicultural practice and evaluation: A case approach to evidence-based practice*. Denver: Love Publishing Company.

Choi, I., J.A. Choi, and A. Norenzayan. 2005. Culture and decisions. In *Blackwell handbook of judgment decision making*, ed. D.J. Koehler and N. Harvey. Malden, Mass.: Blackwell.

Corey, G., M. Corey, and P. Callanan. 2011. *Issues and ethics in the helping professions*. 8th ed. Pacific Grove, Calif.: Brooks/Cole.

Council on Social Work Education (CSWE). 2008. *Educational policy and accreditation standards*. Retrieved April 13, 2010, from http://www.cswe.org/Accreditation/Handbook.aspx?PS=20&layoutChange=Print.

___. 2008. Glossary to *Educational policy and accreditation standards* developed by commission of the Council on Social Work Education. Alexandria, Va.: Council on Social Work Education.

Crestwell, J. and V. Plano-Clark. 2007. *Designing and conducting mixed methods research*. Thousand Oaks, Calif.: Sage.

Day, P.J. 2009. *A new history of social welfare*. 6th ed. Boston: Pearson/Allyn & Bacon.

DeJong, D.H. 2007. Unless they are kept alive: Federal Indian schools and student health. 1878–1918. *American Indian Quarterly* 31(2).

DiNitto, D. M. 2011. *Social welfare: Politics and public policy*. 7th edition. Boston: Pearson Education/Allyn & Bacon.

Dobelstein, A. 1999. *Moral authority, ideology, and the future of American social welfare*. Boulder, CO: Westview Press.

Dolgoff, R., and D. Feldstein. 2009. *Understanding social welfare: A search for social justice*. 8th ed. Boston: Allyn & Bacon.

Dolgoff, R., F.M. Loewenberg, and D. Harrington. 2009. *Ethical decisions for social work practice*. 8th ed. Pacific Grove, Calif.: Cengage Learning.

Dooley, D. 2001. *Social research methods*. 4th ed. Upper Saddle River, NJ: Prentice Hall.

DuBois, B., and K. Miley. 2011. *Social work: An empowering profession*. 7th ed. Boston: Pearson Education/Allyn & Bacon.

Elder Jr., G., and M. Kirkpatrick Johnson. 2003. The life course and aging: Challenges,

lessons, and new directions. In *Invitation to the life course: Toward new understandings of later life*, ed. R. Settersten Jr., 49–81. Amityville, N.Y.: Baywood Publishing Co., Inc.

Engel, R., and R. Schutt. 2009. *The practice of research in social work*. 2nd ed. Thousand Oaks, Calif.: Sage.

Erikson, E. 1963. *Childhood and society*. 2nd ed. New York: W.W. Norton and Company, Inc.

Farley, O., L. Smith, and S. Boyle. 2009. *Introduction to social work*. 11th ed. Boston: Pearson Education/Allyn & Bacon.

Faulkner, C., and S. Faulkner. 2009. *Research methods for social workers: A practice-based approach*. Chicago: Lyceum.

Fischer, J. 1978. *Effective casework practice: An eclectic approach*. New York: McGraw-Hill.

Fischer, J., and K. Corcoran. 2007. *Measures for clinical practice: A sourcebook.* 4th ed. New York: Oxford University Press.

Freud, S. 1920. *A general introduction to psychoanalysis.* New York: Washington Square Press.

Gambrill, E. 2005. *Critical thinking in clinical practice: Improving the quality of judgments and decisions.* Hoboken, N.J.: John Wiley and Sons, Inc.

Garcia-Preto, N. 1996. Puerto Rican families. In *Ethnicity and family therapy,* ed. M. McGoldrick, J. Giordano, and J.K. Pearce, 183–199. New York: Guildford.

Hagestad, G. 2003. Interdependent lives and relationships in changing times: A life-course view of families and aging. In *Invitation to the life course: Toward new understandings of later life,* ed. R. Settersten Jr., 135–159. Amityville, N.Y.: Baywood Publishing Co., Inc.

Hatman, A. 1993. The professional is political. *Social Work* 38:365–366, 504.

Health Care and Education Reconciliation Act, H.R. 4872, 111th Cong., 2nd sess. 2010. Retrieved from Democratic Policy Committee: http://frwebgate.access.gpo.gov/cgi-bin/getdoc.cgi?dbname=111_cong_bills&docid=f:h4872enr.txt.pdf.

Hepworth, D.H., R.H. Rooney, and J. Larsen. 2010. *Direct social work practice: Theory and skills.* 8th ed. Pacific Grove, Calif.: Cengage Learning.

Herrnstein, R., and C. Murray. 1994. *The bell curve: Intelligence and class structure in American life.* New York: Free Press.

Hill, R. 1972. *The Strengths of Black families.* New York: Emerson Hall.

___. 1977. *Informal adoption among Black families.* Washington, D.C.: National Urban League Research Department.

___. 1993. *Research on the African-American family: A holistic perspective.* Westport, Conn.: Auburn House.

___. 1994. The role of the Black church in community and economic development activities. *National Journal of Sociology* 8:149–159.

___. 1999a. *The strengths of African American families: Twenty-five years later.* Lanham, Md.: University Press of America.

___. 1999b. Welfare-to-work legislation: Its impact on children and families. Paper presented to the Delta Research and Educational Foundation Policy Forum, Washington, D.C.

Hodson, G., J. Dovidio, and S. Gaertner. 2004. The aversive form of racism. In *The Psychology of Prejudice,* Vol. 1, ed. Jean Lau Chin, 119–137, 120. Westport, Conn.: Praeger.

Hollis, F. 1964. *Casework: A psychosocial therapy.* New York: Random House.

Hudson, C. 2010. *Complex systems and human behavior.* Chicago: Lyceum.

Hutchison, E. 2008. *Dimensions of human behavior: The changing life course.* 3rd ed. Thousand Oaks, Calif.: Sage.

Jansson, B. 2008. *Becoming an effective policy advocate: From policy practice to social justice.* 5th ed. Belmont, Calif.: Thomson Brooks/Cole.

Jensen, A.R. 1985. The nature of Black-White difference on various psychometric tests: Spearman's hypothesis. *Behavioral and Brain Sciences* 8:193–258.

Jimenez, J. 2010. *Social policy and social change: Toward the creation of social and economic justice.* Los Angeles: Sage.

Karger, H.J. and D. Stoesz. 2010. *American social welfare policy: A pluralist approach.* 6th ed. Boston: Allyn & Bacon

Kirst-Ashman, Karen K. 2007. *Introduction to social work and social welfare: Critical thinking perspectives.* 2nd ed. Belmont, Calif.: Brooks/Cole.

Kohlberg, L. 1981. *The philosophy of moral development.* New York: Harper & Row.

Krysik, J., and J. Finn. 2010. *Research for effective social work practice.* 2nd ed. New York: Routledge.

Leiby, J. 1978. *A history of social welfare and social work in the United States.* New York: Columbia University Press.

Levy, C.S. 1973. The value base of social work. *Journal of Education for Social Work* 9:34–42.

Logan, S.L., ed. 2001. *The Black family: Strengths, self-help, and positive change.* 2nd ed. Boulder, Colo.: Westview Press.

Marczyk, G., D. DeMatteo, and D. Festinger. 2005. *Essentials of research design and methodology.* Hoboken, N.J.: John Wiley & Sons.

McGowan, B.G. 1995. Values and ethics. In *The foundations of social work practice*, ed. C.H. Meyer and M.A. Mattaini. Washington, D.C.: NASW Press.

Midgley, J., and M. Livermore. 2009. *The handbook of social policy*. 2nd ed. Thousand Oaks, Calif.: Sage.

Miley, K.K., M. O'Melia, and B. DuBois. 2011. *Generalist social work practice: An empowering profession*. Updated 6th ed. Boston: Pearson Education/Allyn & Bacon.

Miller, D.C. 1991. *Handbook of research design and social measurement*. Newbury Park, Calif.: Sage.

Miller, H. 1968. Values dilemmas in social casework. *Social Casework* 13:27–33.

Moynihan, D.P. 1965. *The Negro family: The case for national action*. Washington, D.C.: U.S. Department of Labor.

National Association of Social Workers (NASW). Approved 1996, revised 2008. *Code of ethics for social workers*. Washington, D.C.: NASW.

___. 2006. International policy on human rights. In *Social work speaks: NASW policy statements, 2006–2009*. 7th ed. Washington, D.C.: NASW Press.

___. 2006b. *Practice*. Washington, D.C.: NASW Press. Retrieved from http://www.naswdc.org/practice/default.asp.

___. 2008. *Standards for cultural competence*. Retrieved April 15, 2010, from http://www.socialworkers.org/practice/standards/NASWCulturalStandards.pdf.

Netting, F.E., P.M. Kettner, and S.L. McMurtry. 2008. *Social work macro practice*. 4th ed. Boston: Pearson/Allyn & Bacon.

Neuman, W.L., and B. Wiegand. 2000. *Criminal justice research methods*. Boston: Allyn & Bacon.

Newhill, C.E. 1992. Assessing danger to others in clinical social work practice. *Social Service Review* 66(1):64–84.

Newman, B., and P. Newman. 2006. *Development through life: A psychosocial approach*. 9th ed. Belmont, Calif.: Thomson.

Nickerson, R.S. 1986. *Reflections on reasoning*. Hillsdale, N.J.: Erlbaum.

O'Connor, T., D. Hoge, and E. Alexander. 2002. The relative influence of youth and adult experiences on personal spirituality and church involvement. *Journal for the Scientific Study of Religion* 41(4):723–733.

O'Hare, T. 2005. *Evidence-based practices for social workers: An interdisciplinary approach*. Chicago: Lyceum Books, Inc.

Palmiste, C. 2008. Forcible removals: The case of Australian aboriginal and Native American children. *AlterNative: An International Journal of Indigenous Scholarship* 4(2):75–88.

Patient Protection and Affordable Care Act of 2010, H.R. 3590, 111th Cong., 2nd sess. 2010. Retrieved from Democratic Policy Committee: http://dpc.senate.gov/dpcdoc-sen_health_care_bill.cfm.

Patten, M. 2002. *Understanding research methods: An overview of the essentials*. 3rd ed. Los Angeles: Pyrczak Publishing.

Paul, R.W. 1995. *Critical thinking: What every person needs to know how to survive in a rapidly changing world*. Santa Rosa, Calif.: Foundation for Critical Thinking. http://www.criticalthinking.org.

Paul, R.W., and L. Elder. 2006. *Critical thinking: Tools for taking charge of your professional and personal life*. 2nd ed. Upper Saddle River, N.J.: Prentice Hall.

Payne, M. 2006. *What is professional social work?* Chicago: Lyceum Books.

Pinderhughes, E. 1997. Developing diversity competence in child welfare and permanency planning. *Journal of Multicultural Social Work* 5(1/2), 19–38.

Pinderhughes, E.E., K.A. Dodge, J.E. Bates, G.S. Peteit, and A. Zelli. 2000. Discipline responses: Influences of parents' socioeconomic status, ethnicity, beliefs about parenting, stress, and cognitive-emotional processes. *Journal of Family Psychology* 14:380–400.

Popple, P.R., and L. Leighninger. 2011. *The policy-based profession: An introduction to social welfare policy analysis for social workers*. 5th ed. Boston: Allyn & Bacon.

Rappaport, J. 1987. Terms of empowerment/exemplars of prevention: Toward a theory for community psychology. *American Journal of Community Psychology* 15(2):121–144.

Reamer, F.G. 1983. Ethical dilemmas in social work practice. *Social Work* 28:31–35.

___. 1998. The evolution of social work ethics. *Social Work* 43:488–500.

Rhodes, M.L. 1986. *Ethical dilemmas in social work practice*. London: Routledge & Kegan Paul.

Roberts, C.S. 1989. Conflicting professional values in social work and medicine. *Health and Social Work* 14:211–218.

Rogers, A.T. 2006. *Human behavior in the social environment*. New York: McGraw-Hill.

Ross, J.W. 1992. Editorial: Are social work ethics compromised? *Health and Social Work* 17:163–164.

Rubin, A., and E. Babbie. 2008. *Research methods for social work*. 6th ed. Belmont, Calif.: Thompson & Brooks/Cole.

Rutter, M. 1996. Transitions and turning points in developmental psychopathology: As applied to the age span between childhood and mid-adulthood. *International Journal of Behavioral Development* 19(3):603–636.

Saleebey, D. 1996. The strengths perspective in social work practice: Extensions and cautions. *Social Work* 41(3):296–305.

___. 2009. *The strengths perspective in social work practice*. 5th ed. Boston: Pearson Education, Inc.

Schriver, J. 2011. *Human behavior and the social environment: Shifting paradigms in essential knowledge for social work practice*. 5th ed. Boston: Allyn & Bacon.

Schutt, R. 2006. *Investigating the social world*: The process and practice of research. 5th ed. Boston: Sage.

Settersten Jr., R. 2003. Introduction: Invitation to the life course: The promise. In *Invitation to the life course: Toward new understandings of later life*, ed. R. Settersten Jr., 1–12. Amityville, N.Y.: Baywood Publishing Co., Inc.

Staples, R., and L. Johnson. 1993. *Black families at the crossroads: Challenges and prospects*. San Francisco: Jossey-Bass.

Stolzenberg, R., M. Blair-Roy, and L. Waite. 1995. Religious participation in early adulthood: Age and family life cycle effects on church membership. *American Sociological Review* 60:84–103.

Sue, D.W. 2003. *Overcoming our racism: The journey to liberation*. San Francisco: Jossey-Bass.

___. 2006. *Multicultural social work practice*. Hoboken, N.J.: John Wiley & Sons, Inc.

Suppes, M.A., and C.C. Wells. 2009. *The social work experience: An introduction to social work and social welfare*. 5th ed. Boston: Pearson Education/Allyn & Bacon.

Tukey, J.W. 1977. *Exploratory data analysis*. Reading, Mass.: Addison-Wesley.

United Nations. 1948. *Universal Declaration of Human Rights*. Retrieved June 15, 2010, from http://www.un.org/en/documents/udhr/index.shtml.

U.S. Census Bureau. 2010. *State & county Quickfacts: Allegany County*, N.Y. Retrieved June 6, 2010, from http://www.census.gov/newsroom/minority_links/minority_links.html.

Vasquez, M. 1993. The 1992 ethics code: Implications for the practice of psychotherapy. *Texas Psychologist* 45:11.

___. 1994. Implications of the 1992 ethics code for the practice of individual psychotherapy. *Professional Psychology: Research and Practice* 25:321–328.

Vogt, W.P. 2005. *Dictionary of statistics and methodology*. 3rd ed. Newbury Park, Calif.: Sage.

Wakefield, J.C. 1996a. Does social work need the eco-systems perspective? Part 1. Is the perspective clinically useful? *Social Service Review* 70(1):1–32.

Woods, M.E., and F. Hollis. 2000. *Casework: A psychosocial therapy*. New York: McGraw-Hill.

Yamato, G. (1993). Something about the subject makes it hard to name. In V. Cyrus (Ed.) *Experiencing race, class, and gender in the United States* (pp. 206 – 213). Mountain View, CA: Mayfield.

Zastrow, C.H. 2009. *The practice of social work: A comprehensive worktext*. 9th ed. Pacific Grove, Calif.: Cengage Learning.

___. 2010. *Introduction to social work and social welfare: Empowering people*. 10th ed. Belmont, Calif.: Brooks/Cole.

CREDITS

p. 119   Adapted from the National Association of Social Workers. Retrieved from: http://www.naswdc.org/practice/defult.asp

p. 31–32   Dolgoff, R. and Feldstein, D. (2009). *Understanding social welfare: A Search for social justice*. (8th Ed). Boston, MA: Longman Publishing Group.

p. 32   Dolgoff, R. and Feldstein, D. (2009). *Understanding social welfare: A Search for social justice*. (8th Ed). Boston, MA: Longman Publishing Group.

p. 17   DOLGOFF/LOEWENBERG/HARRINGTON. *Ethical decisions for social work practice,* (8th Ed) © 2009 Wadsworth, a part of Cengage Learning, Inc. Reproduced by permission. www.cengage.com/permissions

p. 28–29   Gambrill, Eileen (2006). *Critical thinking in clinical practice: Improving the quality of judgments and decisions*. John Wiley and Sons, Inc.: Hobohen, NJ. Reprinted with permission of John Wiley & Sons, Inc.

p. 42–43   National Association of Social Workers Code of Ethics (2008) and Indicators for the Achievement of the NASW Standards for Cultural Competence in Social Work (NASW, 2007)

p. 119   Reprinted with Permission from the Council on Social Work Education.

p. 121   Saleebey, *Strengths perspective in social work practice,* (5th Ed) excerpts of text from pp. 15–18, © 2009 Allyn & Bacon. Reproduced by permission of Pearson Education, Inc.

p. 94–95   Schriver, *Human behavior & social environment: Shifting paradigms in essential knowledge for social work practice,* (5th Ed). "Kohlberg's Six Stages" from p. 169, © 2011 Pearson Education, Inc. Reproduced by permission of Pearson Education, Inc.